Toronto Reprint Library of Canadian Prose and Poetry

Douglas Lochhead, General Editor

This series is intended to provide for libraries a varied selection of titles of Canadian prose and poetry which have been long out-of-print. Each work is a reprint of a reliable edition, is in a contemporary library binding, and is appropriate for public circulation. The Toronto Reprint Library makes available lesser known works of popular writers and, in some cases, the only works of little known poets and prose writers. All form part of Canada's literary history; all help to provide a better knowledge of our cultural and social past.

The Toronto Reprint Library is produced in short-run editions made possible by special techniques, some of which have been developed for the series by the University of Toronto Press.

This series should not be confused with Literature of Canada: Poetry and Prose in Reprint, also under the general editorship of Douglas Lochhead.

UNIVERSITY OF TORONTO PRESS

Toronto Reprint Library of Canadian Prose and Poetry
© University of Toronto Press 1973
Toronto and Buffalo
Reprinted in paperback 2017
ISBN 978-0-8020-7509-3 (cloth)
ISBN 978-1-4875-9155-7 (paper)

Count Filippo – also published
in 1860 with the joint imprint
of Montreal, E. Dawson & Son;
Toronto, R. & A. Miller 1860.
Title page only varies.

COUNT FILIPPO;

OR,

The Unequal Marriage.

A DRAMA IN FIVE ACTS.

BY THE AUTHOR OF "SAUL."

———◦◦—◦—◦◦———

Montreal:
PRINTED FOR THE AUTHOR; AND FOR SALE AT THE
BOOKSELLERS.
1860.

INTRODUCTION.

~~~~~~~~~~

NEXT in enormity to a breach of the marriage relation, stands its mutual contraction by youth and years. To give a truthful, though fictitious, instance of the sad issue of such an ill-omened union as the latter, is the aim of this drama.

PERSONS REPRESENTED.

TREMONLA, *Duke of Pereza; a very aged Sovereign.*

HYLAS, *his youthful son, and only child.*

COUNT FILIPPO, *an elderly Nobleman, and Chief Minister of State.*

SERAPHIO, *friend of Count Filippo.*

GONARDO, *a Perezan gentleman whose estate joins that of Count Filippo;
   and who, during the play, is generally disguised as a gypsy.*

FIDEO, *Secretary of the Duke.*

GALLANTIO, *a disreputable Noble of Pereza.*

VERTALDI, *a Perezan Noble.*

MARCO,
PISANIO, } *Gentlemen of Count Filippo's suite.*

DUKE OF ARNO.

VOLINA, *the youthful lady of Count Filippo.*

PAPHIANA, *wife of Gonardo.*

A LADY *of the Court of Pereza.*

LORDS, SENATORS, COURTIERS, OFFICERS, SERVANTS, &c.

COUNT FILIPPO.

ACT I.

SCENE I.

An Apartment in the Ducal Palace of Pereza. The Duke *seated in an easy chair.* Hylas *standing near.*

HYLAS.

What needs this haste to marry me? I cannot
Love, more than hate, at pleasure. 'T were as cruel
Toward Arno's ducal daughter as toward me,
Thus, with stern Hymen's so potential chains,
To bind her steadfast heart, to one whom you
Full oft declare capricious as a vane.

DUKE.

Oh, speak not now of that. Thou wilt amend;
When wed, wilt lose thy wandering regard.
Her eyes shall fix thine, as the cynosure
Doth fix the steady steering mariner's.—
But bid Gallantio now keep aloof:
Though he hath stained thy youth, it is not meet
He should bedaub and smear thy married life.
Let him retire from court, or, even yet,
He shall be punished.—Speak not for him, Hylas;
Do thou not intercede for that fallen peer,

B

That Belial of Pereza, who no more
Can from his fault's depths rise into our favor,
Than, from his pit, can Lucifer to heaven.

HYLAS.

'Tis Filippo incenses you against him.

DUKE.

No, from that quarter bloweth not the wind.
Count Filippo's words have merely been the echo
Of our own judgment's loud denouncing tongue.
Why dost thou look askance on Filippo?
Hylas, he is indeed thy guardian angel,
Loving thee more (and that in truth is much)
Than he abhors the vile Gallantio.—
Lo, here he comes.

[*Enter* FILIPPO.

Count, when do you depart
To Arno, on our son's love-embassy?

FILIPPO.

To morrow, if it so shall please your highness.

DUKE.

'Tis well, 'tis well.—Pray bring your wife to court
When you return.   We see by far too little
Of face as fair as is the front of heaven.

FILIPPO.

Thanks to your goodness.

DUKE.

We grow foolish, though,
Desiring to cull flowers, when these eyes
Must perish sooner than the painted petals.
Still let her come.   How know we but ourselves
May shuffle through a gentle measure with her,
At Hylas' nuptials; that these stiff limbs,
Scorning this long-kept, stationary seat,
As icicles touched by a sudden shaw,
Drop from th' eaves and, all dissolved, along

Dance, mingling with the glittering, rippling rills,
May take a trice, afresh, the festal floor ?
But we do doat, fond that we are, thus weak.
Lend me your arms.

              [HYLAS *and* FILIPPO *assist the* DUKE *to rise.*

              Now lead me to my room :
This chair less grateful is than my left couch.
What am I but an old, exhausted man,
Nigh bedridden ?   Our voice now only scares
The doctor and the nurse ; though once, when heard
Upon the doubtful and contested field,
While it established ours, made shake the foe.
But we are shorn down by these crescent moons,
Life-reaping sickles ; we whom war hath spared,
(And spare us yet a little, Chronos' scythe !)
Must soon by death, the tireless husbandman,
Be cast as hay upon the stack of time ;
Garnered, must soon, a scar, surviving blade,
Lie in the wintry storehouse of the grave.
Lay us upon our couch again : so, so.
Ah, is this tottering all that life hath left ?
Hylas, thou seest what thyself shalt be.
Still, let us see thee married ere we die,
And we leave life without complaint, regret.
Lead to our closet ; there we count our beads.
This form full soon must wear the coffin's weeds.

                                     [*Exeunt.*

SCENE II.

Library of Count Filippo's mansion, near Pereza.   FILIPPO *and* VOLINA.

VOLINA.

Call me capricious, fanciful, whate'er
You choose : it matters not.—What though I have
Whims, are not wives allowed to have them now ?
Nay, if you shake your head, I'll say 'tis naught
When you do kiss and tell me that you love me.

FILIPPO.

But this is such a singular desire;
Stranger than strange hath hitherto conceived,
Or traveller yet told.—Nay, sweet Volina,
Ask me for something that may be obtained.

VOLINA.

Obtain me something that will never weary.
I'm tired of that green parroquet's harsh cry;
That English lark's rich song now makes me drowsy.
My lute seems cracked; those songs you brought me, stupid.
Bring me a mocking-bird, or catch me th' Huma.

FILIPPO.

The Huma lights not, nor thy fancy long.
Volina, what are parrots and caged larks;
What were a whole aviary of Humas,
What lute, what songs; what were the Halcyon,
Though it were thine, did it divide thy breast
With that young brooding vulture discontent?

VOLINA.

Who would not brood? You keep no company;
I seldom see the world, the court now never.
None do I see save you, nought do I hear
Save mine own voice, with wind through sighing trees,
The hum of flies, unmeaning notes of birds,
And the wild glee (I envy) of my maids;—
And now more than a month you may be hence.

FILIPPO.

And will that longer seem to thee than me,
Who fly into thine arms as dove to cote,
Impatient for the eve as dove for dawn?
Peace, peace: frequent this library, where holds
The levee of the monarchs of our race.
Unable to converse with me, come here
And speak with the great spirits of the past.

VOLINA.

Here do I often come when you are absent,
But cannot aye be entertained with ghosts.
I've read the poets through, and files of fiction ;
And what to me are law, philosophy?
What all your dead historians' ink-brains?
I'm sick of sun and solitude and books,
Sick of new robes, and dumb, though shining, jewels.—
Take me with you to Arno.

FILIPPO.

Dear, I cannot.

VOLINA.

Then leave me at the court with old Tremohla,
Who still has sought of you my long-due visit,
Which you have still with some excuse postponed.

FILIPPO.

Keep house, Volina, until I return ;
When, if success attend upon this suit,
Beauty, like jewels, will be in demand,
To grace the gorgeous nuptials of the prince ;
And thou, my jewel, that hath long been hid
Within this sober casket of my home,
Brighter, because a stranger, forth shalt come.
Art thou content?

VOLINA.

'T would seem I must be so.

FILIPPO.

Nay, all so sullen, girl ?   Is this our parting ?

VOLINA.

Return you to the city ere you start
Upon your amorous embassy to Arno ?

FILIPPO.

I do ; and now, without extravagance,
Inform me, sweet, what thence to bring for thee.

VOLINA.

Bring me four men to dig me a dry-well,
From whence the stars may be observed by day:
That were some change.   I'll turn astronomer;
Measure Orion's belt, ogle Arcturus,
Play with the Pleiades, romp with the bear,
And wink again at every winking star.
Heighe! would I were in the north star now!

FILIPPO.

As Jason fetched the golden fleece from Colchis,
So I would thee from that cold, silvery world.—
I would thou went that I might fetch thee thence.

VOLINA.

I would that I were in the golden sun!

FILIPPO.

That doth remind me of a sun-like steed,
The hue of gold, that lately I beheld,
Whose cantering hoofs, as they did scour the road,
Shod as with silver, seemed four dancing stars,—
A Pegasus indeed, except for wings;
And, as I gazed admiringly, methought
That thou upon its back wouldst seem a muse.
It shall be thine, Vol; so that I, when thou
Dismount'st therefrom into mine arms at eve,
May deem thee fragrant from the hill of heaven,
All fresh and dewy from the shining clouds.
Kiss, and good morrow until evening shrouds.

[*Kisses her passionately and exit.*

VOLINA.

Would I too were a man like Filippo,
To mount, and, lover-like, in boots and spurs,
Rush into the great city's open arms!
The country is a dull old-fashioned maid,
Well enough, truly, for wild, wayward children,
As is a spinster aunt to care for them,

But when these children are grown men and women,
They will be governed by the aunt no more.
I'm weary of these grave, environing woods,
'Midst which I dwell and watch the wandering clouds,
Until I yearn to wander after them.
Ah, me! what task shall I betake me to?
I've no delight now in embroidery,
Nor music, save 'tis in the minor mode;
Nor books, my husband's panacea, save
To scrawl upon their margins serious sonnets.
I would I were a man like Filippo!
Heigho! he'd take me to the court, he said,
(And may it be early!) when the prince is wed.

[*Exit.*

SCENE III.

Within the Ducal Palace at Pereza. HYLAS *and* GALLANTIO.

HYLAS.

Consent I will not, though to please the Duke;
To whom, besides a subject's, as my sire,
I owe to yield a son's allegiance.

GALLANTIO.

Indeed 'tis hard to wed you in such haste.

HYLAS.

I will not marry yet; I'm absolute
In this, as is my father in all else.

GALLANTIO.

It is too early, and exceeding harsh
So soon to clip your amour-bearing wings.

HYLAS.

Was not my sire himself a bachelor
At sixty-five? and I at twenty, lo!
Am threatened with the noose!

GALLANTIO.

To hang yourself therein were better deed.
Take sick and die,—or say you are impotent.

HYLAS.

The Duke doth deem this match will cage me up.
Affection for this yet unseen princess,
As the court tailor's shears shape cloth of gold,
Cut my career to Hymen's current mode.

GALLANTIO.

A garment that himself abhorred to wear!
Your father set the fashion in Pereza,
Of a celibate life.   More bachelors,
More merry dogs, have barked at Cerberus,
Since the accession of Tremohla, than
Of married have paid fee unto Saint Peter.
But, as we said, the old Duke feels his end,
And matrimony is a gulf that you
Must leap into for his sake and Pereza's,
Even as into dim and fabulous chasm
Horatio Cocles leaped for good of Rome.

HYLAS.

We will not leap as yet, for any's good;
Would disobey though thrice he were our sire.

GALLANTIO.

I'd never call him sire again, but grandsire.
To spend your life in his? to seize upon
Your years' reversion!   Like the prodigal,
He hath not stayed at home, see, in his own life,
But gone into the far country of yours,
And, with the tusk of foul concupiscence,
Crunched up your pleasant acorns, leaving you,
In being's trough, only some marriage husks,
To be digested, as you'll find, with pain.

HYLAS.

It maddens me!

GALLANTIO.

Mad? marry, I should rave.
He made the heir after disinheriting him.
Your father mortgaged you before your birth ;
Pledged you unto his pleasures, long before
He pledged his faith in wedlock to your mother ;
You now are claimed as forfeit to be sold :—
But Filippo doth hurry you to the mart.

HYLAS.

Count Filippo himself did shew no haste
Fulfil the fruitful function, wedding late.

GALLANTIO.

And yet to little purpose ;—for his lady,
Is she not childless, bringing him no heir?

HYLAS.

I see it all, I see it in its source !
My father like a catterpillar hath eaten,
In his decline, the green leaf of my days :
I was defrauded ere my birth by his
Dishonestly prolonged celibacy.

GALLANTIO.

Ten years he, brazen-helmeted, served Mars,
Then should have donned the donkey-cap of hymen,
In lieu whereof he thirty summers served
Venus, whose wars result in life, not death.
At length, much more from policy than choice,
He volunteered to serve just one campaign,
Under the god that floats the saffron flag ;
When, even as an old recruiting sergeant
Into some sleeping youth's palm slips the shilling,
Enlists he you, while you (Heaven knows where) slept.

HYLAS.

Yet kinder parent never cherished child,—
Indulgent even to excess indeed,
Mindful to please me now, when most he's stern.
'Tis said this princess is a paragon.

GALLANTIO.

So are all maidens until they are married.
Think you the father will inform the suitor
His daughter is a dolt, a vixen? no, no more
Than to the young aspirant to a saddle
Will the horsedealer say the mare is spavined.
But mark, in this I most blame Filippo.

HYLAS.

Between ourselves, I too.

GALLANTIO.

                    Oh, 'tis most wrong;
Unwarrantable, calling for reproof,—
Nay, indignation,—yes, and for revenge.

HYLAS.

For it I bear him secretly great grudge.

GALLANTIO.

Although your father anvil is and hammer,
He is the fire at forging of these chains.

HYLAS.

I know it.

GALLANTIO.

He moves Tremohla to this marriage mischief.

HYLAS.

He doth : I have perceived it.

GALLANTIO.

                    And to think,
Moreo'er, that fortune should deal so perversely;
To think a man of temper so austere,
Enjoys such superfluity of bliss.
Have you not marked his lady? 'tis a woman
Meet for a Moorish monarch in his pride;
In one fair alabaster honey-cup,
Enough to sate a sultan's appetite.

HYLAS.

I once beheld her.

GALLANTIO.
     And not coveted ?
Her face is as a list to tempt gay knights.

HYLAS.
That I then thought unhallowedly I own,
Knowing, as we did, that she was Filippo's,
And longed to vault into his rosy bed.

GALLANTIO.
Love's rosy gauntlet lies upon her cheek,
And were I Hylas I would take it up.
What fear you Filippo's tilting ? 'Tis not strange
That he so seldom brings her to the court.
She cannot love him, more than day loves night :—
She should be woo'ed by night, for she by day
Would be too dazzling ; and she pours her voice
Charmed o'er the lips to the saluted ear,
Soft as the brooklet's sounding 'neath the sedge,
Or overflowing fountain heard by night.
She sings divinely as the nightingale,
Dances with grace beyond Terpsichore.
To have seen her not, is not to have seen the sun ;
To have missed her motion, to have missed the moon's,
Or mounting morning's going up the skies.
She seems, beneath her cope of sable hair,
Aurora underneath dark cope of clouds ;
Appears to step as on the waving wind,
On moving make a chariot of the air.

HYLAS.
This were to be perfection.

GALLANTIO.
     Nothing lacks she
Of form, or feature, voice, to take the court,
To the uttermost accomplished : yet at home
All lonely she abides as nested thrush ;
Save when she, mounted, wildly gallops forth,
To take the air, or fling herself abroad,
Skimming the lea as skims the lake the swallow.

HYLAS.

Poor lady! why is this?   Can Filippo
Enact the jailor on the innocent?

GALLANTIO.

She is believed to be o'er amorous;
Myself have seen her underneath his nose,
Shoot glances, to the hearts of gallants fatal
As were Apollo's arrows to the Python;
Herself a gorgeous snake, a charming dragon,
And, were I Hylas, I would act Saint George,
Encountering her, and, for the feat, hereafter
Be canonized by Venus' loving church.

HYLAS.

'T were fraught with too much peril.

GALLANTIO.

                    Peril? pish!
Is that a word for sovereigns?

HYLAS.

                 I believe her
Pure as a perfect lily.

GALLANTIO.

              Am I, then,
A novice in my knowledge of the signs
That prove a lover's loophole in a woman?
Believe these lips,—assuredly from hers
Hopeless of favors, and that would not take
One florin from her reputation's worth,
But rather coin for her a mint of merit,—
She is a landscape, wrapped indeed in snow,
But, underneath, the heated, golden mine.

HYLAS.

I'm half resolved.

GALLANTIO.

Resolve you all.

HYLAS.

               And yet—

GALLANTIO.

Shake not your head.

HYLAS.

She may be wise as fair.

GALLANTIO.

There's no abyss so wide as woman's folly;
'T would take this world in, then hold such another.

HYLAS.

But Filippo, my father's minister,—
Consider him, his worth, his weight, his years.

GALLANTIO.

Doth he consider you ? doth he not seek
To stem and turn your youth's full, forward flood,
And burst its silvery bubbles of delight,
By damming it in marriage' stagnant pool ?
Yea, in your very blossom to uproot you,
And pitch you like a faggot to the fiends.

HYLAS.

Too true, too true.

GALLANTIO.

He doth officiously to Arno wend,
Striving, with hymeneal ivy dark,
To bind and blight the stout oak of your life.

HYLAS.

He doth, he doth.

GALLANTIO.

Hie you where his own honeysuckle blooms.

HYLAS.

Methinks we will.

GALLANTIO.

You shall be sweetbriar to her twining arms.

HYLAS.

Think'st so ?

GALLANTIO.

To hers he is but as the pricking thorn.

HYLAS.

He doth prick me;—scarce yet to life enlarged,
Is seeking now, with most remorseless speed,
To clap me into wedlock's narrow cell.

GALLANTIO.

Plunder the constable.

HYLAS.

He were well served.

GALLANTIO.

With counterfeit of wedlock's ivory key,
Enter his house while he is gone abroad.
Be you a stinging wasp within his hive,
A fly within his larder.

HYLAS.

So I will.

GALLANTIO.

While he is fishing in the brook at Arno,
Do you prepare and fill at home your net.

HYLAS.

Why not? others have had their fish caught.

GALLANTIO.

Ay,
And fried too; therefore why should you forbear?
Plant yourself by his wife; before her eyes
Play the Adonis, play Sir Hyacinth;
Display your person and accomplishments;
Throw all your jets into the sunny air,
Till thirst itself be bred at sight of drink,
As thirst is bred by drinking of the sea;
Admire her until she admire again,
As sound makes echo, or as one struck string
To other, chordant, with low breath responds;
Drink from her eyes till she with her regards
Comes like a fawn to slake herself at yours.

HYLAS.

I'll strive to draw her to the brink o'the brook:
'T were pleasant play the wolf with such a lamb.

GALLANTIO.

Startle her not. Be subtle as the snake;
Gentle, albeit bold. From coral cup
Still let her drink the wine of flattering lips.

HYLAS.

Teach me no longer, but inform me how
I may obtain an introduction to her.

GALLANTIO.

Methinks you know Seignior Gonardo's lady.

HYLAS.

You know her if report speaks truly.

GALLANTIO.

She hath the ear of Filippo's fair wife,
And shall invite her to her house to night,
Where you and I, as if by chance, will meet her.

HYLAS.

Away: I grow impatient there to greet her.

GALLANTIO.

Shall we together ?

HYLAS.

　　　　　　　　　　No, I go before :—
The prim old world doth watch us more and more.
　　　　　　　　　　　　　　[*Exit.*

GALLANTIO.

Now shall the he-goat black adultery,
With the roused ram retaliation, twine
Their horns in one, to butt at Filippo!
I hate him for his frequent, stern rebukes,
And counselling the Duke to banish me.
Shall I not pierce him in the side, betray him
With this young Judas of a prince's kiss ?
Go on before, young Duke elect, and fear
The prim old world: ha, ha, ha, did I hear?

END OF THE FIRST ACT.

ACT II.

SCENE I.

An Apartment in Filippo's mansion. VOLINA *and* PAPHIANA.

PAPHIANA.

Shoot from thy sphere, my pale and fixèd star,
And come revolve within my heavens to night.

VOLINA.

Here are my heavens. Though dull, I have resolved,
In my lord's absence, to abide at home.

PAPHIANA.

Nay, speak not so : I shall take no denial.
Pray visit me. A palace were a prison,
Did still its inmates keep within the walls.
Dull is the owl, but you are even duller ;—
At least, she plies the downy wing at dusk.
Your lord were glad : pray come this evening.
Till he returns, make much with me your home.

VOLINA.

You are most kind, albeit now excuse me :
Till he returns I play the coy recluse.

PAPHIANA.

Are you, then, so in love with solitude ?
You cloud up far too much your sunny face
In these umbrageous precincts, shining but
By night, and in the presence of your spouse,
When you with watching pale are as the moon,
And, from the situation of your chair,
Do meet his drowsy gazes. Pardon me,
You are too young, and, surely, far too fair,

To bo alivo (as I affirm you are)
Within this mausoleum mansion buried.

VOLINA.

I ride abroad.

PAPHIANA.

And what is riding, pray,
With but the shadow of a distant groom?
Love, like a shadow, vanishes at last
For object ever absent. It is man,
Not horse, you want,—a lover in a husband.
Wherefore does yours not squire you through the glades?
Pleasure is doubled when the donor's pleased:
But for a double pleasure where were th' world?
That is renewed in mutual delight.

VOLINA.

Fie! madam;—see my new-bought palfrey.

PAPHIANA.

[having advanced towards, and looking through, the window.

Ah,

Pretty enough. I'm no equestrian:
I'd rather roll in Phaeton's gilded car,
Than track the sky upon Bellerophon.

VOLINA.

To-morrow it shall shew me all its paces:—
It is the very courser for a sylph.
Its back appears a burnished bridge of gold.
Hear how in pride of form and hue it treads
Out merry music in the pebbled court.
Methinks it moves with arched and swaying neck,
As a gay gondola might tilting go
Over the Adriatic in a breeze.
Was it not kind of Filippo to buy it?

PAPHIANA.

What could he less than buy you anything?
He who, to please the old, eccentric Duke,

C

Doth spend his presence, which is your estate,
Perpetually with musty senators,
And with whom else uncertain, leaving you
Meanwhile to hold the empty purse of absence.

VOLINA.

Nay, nay, I find you too injurious.
Not from his choice, but at Tremohla's wish,
And for Pereza's weal, doth Filippo
Stint me his company; while this long absence
Comes not of search for his mere proper pleasure,
But Hylas' weal, and Hylas' pleasure too,
Since great the fame of Arno's Ducal maid.

PAPHIANA.

Ah, you have struck upon the current theme!
There's many a maiden in Pereza dying
This hour for Hylas,—widows too and wives.
No wonder the wet nymphs caressed his namesake,
If that were half so beautiful as this.

VOLINA.

Widows and wives are dying for him? Oh!

PAPHIANA.

Are we immortal for that we are wed?
Doth marriage make us proof 'gainst Cupid's bolt?
Can whiskers pall us for a downy cheek?
I hate old men, whose porcupinal beards
Prick, grizzled, like that creature's speckled quills;
And would as leave take kisses from a hedgehog,
Or seek for drink, when thirsty, from a well
Guarded by thistles, as beseech such lips.

VOLINA.

But to be married is to shut the door
On such conceits, or to expel them from us.

PAPHIANA.

We married women should have given in charge
The single men, since we the art of love

Could teach them better than a hundred Ovids.
As veterans are chosen to instruct
The raw recruit in future use of arms,
So should we each have given a youth in charge.
I would teach Hylas free of cost.
I would I were the mother of the cub,
That I might hug him almost to the death!
Think, weave one's fingers in his amber hair;
To kiss him even till he pouted, then
To kiss him till he smiled, and then
With kissing make him pout and smile again.

VOLINA.

Is he so wonderous beautiful?

PAPHIANA.

The sweetest youth seen since Narcissus drowned him.
He is that most equivocal, sweet thing,
Nor youth nor man, but just the best of both.
My lord grows old like yours doth, but young Hylas
Just coming up time's hill!—Oh, to waylay him,
As Venus did Adonis!

VOLINA.

Hear, Gonardo!

PAPHIANA.

He cannot: he is travelling for his health.

VOLINA.

Where?

PAPHIANA.

Nay I know not.   Would he were
In heaven quietly.   All have their bitters;—
Yes, and some have theirs brewed and they not know it.
You know the catch:

[Sings.

Marriage is a cup of gall,
Brewed by crafty priest and sire,—
Bitter, bitter, very bitter;
Who in drinking does not tire?

Girl, I believe my spouse is false to me,
Since every man is a born libertine.

VOLINA.

No, for my husband to his vow is true.

PAPHIANA.

Where all are false, yours is as true as any.
Being true as wind within the variables,
He keeps at least his secret concubine.

VOLINA.

Would you impugn my lord's fidelity?

PAPHIANA.

Ah, now I see you're jealous:—but no matter;
Herein all husbands would deceive their wives.
Doubtless yours loves you, yet imagine not
In Arno he not seeks, in love's alembic,
To turn to silver hours the iron night.
Nay, wherefore look so strange?

VOLINA.

                    Your words are strange.

PAPHIANA.

But true.—Zounds! it would make me vow, at night
To imitate that meek, mock maid the moon,
When circumstance comports with secrecy,
And slumber with some fair Endymion.
What are you looking at?

VOLINA.

                    My palfrey yonder.

PAPHIANA.

See how it paws!

VOLINA.

                    Have patience, my sweet steed.

PAPHIANA.

Even as yon groom restrains that pawing mare,
So would our liege lords hold us hard in hand.—

But will you come and visit me to night ?
You shall find with me our most dainty prince.

VOLINA.

Ah, then the god you spoke of is your guest !
Comes he alone ?

PAPHIANA.

No ; with a cavalier,
The most accomplished in all Italy.

VOLINA.

Expect me not.

PAPHIANA.

Indeed I shall. Fond woman,
Do not perversely disappoint yourself.
Pray be advised ; let me implore,
Even entreat, your coming as a boon.

VOLINA.

Entreat me not.

PAPHIANA.

I shall take no denial.—
Nay, get you to a nunnery at once ;
A cloister were best place for mortifying,
For pinching pleasure out of the proud flesh.
But why should pleasure either pine or pinch ?
Why saints wear sackcloth and be solitary ?
To-night come to my sanctuary, sister,
And, casting off this sackcloth coyness, play
Thy part now with my pair of merry monks.

VOLINA.

No further importune me.

PAPHIANA.

Be admired :
Look into this dumb glass, that cannot flatter
And see as you are seen by others' eyes.

VOLINA.

You cannot tempt me, so but lose your breath.

PAPHIANA.

You lose much, thus sequestered.   Oh, had I
Those luciferian, archangelic eyes,
Wore I such brilliants in my brow, such beacons
Upon my headland, two such Hero love-lights,
Hung out by nature for Leander's view,
Tempters to light even such another two,—

VOLINA.

Fie! fie! this flattery fulsome is as foul.
I pay no visits till the Count returns.

PAPHIANA.

No?

VOLINA.

No.

PAPHIANA.

You hold to that bad mind?

VOLINA.

I do.

PAPHIANA.

Why then farewell.   But you may yet grow tired
Of hiding here, unnoted, unadmired.

[Exit.

VOLINA.

Loose words imply loose thoughts.   Woe to her spouse,
Such conversation heralding such guests:
The prince as wild as is a hare in March,
The gayest of the gallants of the time.
And who is this accomplished cavalier?
It cannot be Gallantio; the same
That leads, 'tis said, his highness into evil;
Discreditable amours, play immense;
So deep and frequent, Filippo declares,
'T would soon leave void Pereza's full exchequer.
I fear Gonardo's sky looks scowlingly:
Therein there seems no music of the spheres,
But gathering thunder, rain of torrent tears.
Veiled lightnings lurk on those lascivious lips,

And zigzag will return one day to pierce her,
Taming those eyes of hers, than lightnings fiercer.
No, better here in dull and plaintive plight,
Than gaily shining in her heavens to night.

[*Exit.*

SCENE II.

Within Gonardo's house. Enter GALLANTIO *and* PAPHIANA.

GALLANTIO.

What, pouting, Paph? come, purr a little, puss.
Was the incomparable countess gracious?
Will she consort with us? sweet sybil, say.

PAPHIANA.

Why have you sent me on a barren errand?
I go no more to see the faithful fool,
Who would not listen to my invitation,
But had resolved, till Filippo's return,
To pay no visits, see no company.

GALLANTIO.

Despite of her resolve, she shall see Hylas.
Believe me, Paph, never astronomer
Waited more eagerly for rising star,
Than he this evening waits this paragon,
Whom he believes is now beneath this roof.
They must be face to face before the moon
Doth rise to night and face the dusky earth.
I pray thee aid me to thine uttermost
To intersect their orbits with each other.

PAPHIANA.

I see not how. To force an interview
Might much offend her, and all foully mar
What you would wish to see so fairly made.

GALLANTIO.

The prince is confident; expects much joy.

PAPHIANA.

The prince had better not expect too much.

GALLANTIO.

He plays the burglar wheresoe'er he goes,
Entering the heart at window of the eye,
As sunbeams at a chink.   He shall possess her.

PAPHIANA.

Shall!
Oh, great assurance! she is not so callow
As is your confident and downy Dukeling,
Who must go round about if he'd approach her,
And scare her not into a thicker brake.
Is this his first bird-nesting?—oh, I would
She were an eagle to pick out his eyes!

GALLANTIO.

How now?

PAPHIANA.

You men think every woman
A barn-door fowl, and every man a falcon.

GALLANTIO.

Nay, be not angry, love, to night.   Peace, peace:
Passion doth make thee ugly.

PAPHIANA.

I am vexed;—
But listen, and applaud a happy thought.

GALLANTIO.

What is it, Paph?

PAPHIANA.

I spy another spray,
Whereon to-morrow she will proudly perch;
Whence, as the thoughtless songster, 'midst the leaves,
Eddies into the armed, distended jaws

Of the coiled serpent gazing from the root,
She may, into young Hylas' open arms,
Swoon down from her allegiance to her lord.

GALLANTIO.

How?

PAPHIANA.

She is now possessed of a rare palfrey,
On which to-morrow she will take the air,
Let the prince then encounter her.   Is 't well?

GALLANTIO.

Most excellent.   Lend me a few more ducats.
Hylas shall, mounted, meet her on the road.—
Lend me two hundred ducats.

PAPHIANA.

Curb thine extravagance, Gallantio.
Say for what end thou ask'st again for ducats.

GALLANTIO.

Meddle not now with family affairs.
Thou art my duck, and ducats are duck's children.
When we are married, all our darling ducats
Shall in one purse and pen cry " Quack, quack, quack!"
Lend me two hundred ducats.   May I die
Myself, instead of sick Gonardo, now,
If I should play thee false with kiss or cash.
'T is for a wager with the prince, dear Paph.

PAPHIANA. [giving him a purse.

This purse contains your sum.   But ask no more;—
Indeed, this borrowing doth make me poor.

GALLANTIO.

Now to the prince.   Adieu!—Why, how is this
That thou o hold'st me anchored with thine eyes?—
Yet must I leave thee, must now cast thee off.

PAPHIANA.

You will return.

GALLANTIO.

Ay, that I will to-morrow.

PAPHIANA.

To-morrow? if thou art not here before
Old Time doth pass his foot o'er midnight's brow,
Thy foot shall never pass my threshold more.
To-morrow? is to-morrow lover's time?
The lover's hour is the perpetual now.—
But get thee gone.

[*Exit* GALLANTIO.

I love too much yon fascinating fool,
Compound of fat and frolic.   I must cool,
Else he may lose some ardour.—O, to-morrow!
Ha, ha, ha, ha!
To-morrow shall Volina, luck betiding,
Encounter Hylas on the road a-riding.

SCENE III.

A Chamber in the Ducal Palace.   The DUKE *and* HYLAS.

HYLAS.

Why is your highness still incensed against me?

DUKE.

We still must chide, for that Gallantio
Is a black blot and blur upon thy life.
Purge thyself from him, pluck him off thee now,
Else we will banish him while we do live;
He who himself hath half of his estate
Confiscated to gamesters, and the rest
Squanders on bawds and bullies.—Heaven forgive me,
I know not why I've let the foul frog float
In the same waters with thy tadpole state.
Command him thence; let him no longer, Hylas,
Haunt the clear wave of thy connubial days.

But we perceive that thou dost not regard us:
Thou art impatient to begone to him.
Undutcous, go; thou wilt not stay by me.
Thou mayest remember this when I am gone.
We have not many days to stay on earth.

HYLAS.

Your highness, in your ill-construing ire,
Mistakes my purpose: I but wished to ride.

DUKE.

Then go: we are content. But ere thou goest,
Come nearer us, and lift thy sullen brow,
Or we shall say, what we almost believe,
This Arno's daughter is too good for thee.

[HYLAS approaches.

Look on us, Hylas, whom we look upon
Out of this body of bedarkened age,
As might the old moon look upon the young,
When, dwindled doubtful to obliterate shade,
It vague sits gazing, with a lorn regard,
Into the latter's shining circlet face.
Thou dost succeed us in Pereza's throne,
As in the sky the new moon doth the old.
Govern here wisely; nor by word, as deed,
Within the pregnant confines of the state,
That now of Arno is in labor's throes,
Stint marriage of the dues of early days.
Ah, therein I and Filippo have failed!
So wilt not thou, but wilt dry up one source
Of dire domestic ill. Herein not fail;
Nor fail, we charge thee by a father's love,
Hylas, henceforth to cherish Filippo,
And from thy favor spurn Gallantio:—
Thou wert seen with him even yesterday.

HYLAS. [aside.

What prying ghost beheld us and informed?

DUKE.

Deny it not: a bird sang such a tune.
No more behold that peccant peer, we pray thee,
If thou wouldst have thy father die in peace.
We are but ill at ease: come, Filippo.—
Hylas, our heart keeps life till his return,
As lamp keeps light within a Roman tomb.
When he returns methinks we shall expire,
As with the opened tomb the lamp's lent fire.
Now forth to ride. Ah me, so fails our force,
When we next ride 't must be on death's pale horse.
Let me lean on thee, boy.

> [*Having risen and leaning on* HYLAS.

           Thus leaks out life,
As spirit from an old and crazy cask;
But a more flask-full now left in this head;
In trunk and limbs the old tree well nigh dead.

> [*Exeunt, the* DUKE *leaning on the prince.*

SCENE IV.

A Corridor in the Ducal Palace. Time, dusk.

GALLANTIO.   [*Pacing to and fro.*

[*The clock of the Palace Tower strikes.*]

Seven mortal hours!—and yet it seems much more.
Come, Hylas, come; waylayer of woman, scion
Of a libidinous stock. Oh, fair the stock
On which thou'dst graft! Forgive me, mother Venus,
For not attempting this exploit myself;
But in thy service I have been so long
Such a marauder and bold buccaneer,
That, saving Paph's one proud peninsula,
'Gainst my descents the whole wide coast of woman
Seems armed and fortified.

> [*Enter* HYLAS *at the end of the corridor.*

Now, merry Bacchus, here my sweet ghost comes!
The rose of joy upon his cheek, and bright

His eye with risen star of satisfaction.—
How hath your highness sped?

CENTER>HYLAS.

Sped? O Gallantio, I almost fear
Fortune hath been too kind, and lures me on
To dash and to disgrace me! We have met.

GALLANTIO.

And how hath she received you?

HYLAS

With drooped head:

Till, as a youthful bather, having dived,
Shining emerges fairer from the wave,
So showed her blushing cheeks and conscious eyes.
O, knew I not till then how fair was woman!
And silently I worshipped her; and still
Mute gazed upon her, knowing not I gazed;
Holding her hand, to which mine seemed to grow.

GALLANTIO.

'T was well: the touch is love's electric line.

HYLAS.

I love her!

GALLANTIO.

She shall you.—What next ensued?

HYLAS.

As trees from either margin of a stream,
All overhanging in a long embrace,
Mingle their branches, so our fingers twined;
Till, ending that sweet impropriety,
She did the soft entanglement undo:
Then, having to my prayer to be her squire
Vouchsafed a chaste consent, we rode away,
Now chatting loud, now fallen to tones love-low;
When suddenly, by fear or frolic seized,
Her nag, a tawny palfrey, with her flew,
With all the roses blowing from her cheeks,

Soon like white daisied downs, or as if wrapped
In envious winding-sheet, or death had come
Urging behind, damp breathing on life's flame,
She fading as a taper in the socket,
And reeling on her seat; whence now I snatched,
And bore her safely to mine own stout steed;
That careful through the winding leafy lane,
As freighted argosy through narrow seas,
Steered as it knew how precious was its burden;
Myself, dismounted, walking by her side,
Rejoicing towards her home, whereat arrived,
She bade me enter,—what could she do less?
Which I did do,—what could I wish for more?

GALLANTIO.

You are the pet of every prurient god!
Fortune hath been unblindfolded to-day,
And turned her wheel adroitly; you shall ride
Soon on its highest spoke. See her again
To-morrow; you are free now of her house;
This accident occasion being and screen,
Behind which you may with her play the fool.
See her again; Count Filippo will thank you,
And from this hour among his dear friends rank you.
Why are you silent? is it not even so?

HYLAS.

We fear, though stands ajar her honor's door,
The winking mastiff virtue cowers behind it.

GALLANTIO.

Fear not; advance, albeit on cautious steps.
Although a robber, look the honest man.
The time is brief, so make what haste you can.
Now get to bed, and dream of this till day.
Good night. I by the postern will away.

[*Exeunt separately.*

SCENE V.

A noble apartment in Filippo's mansion. Through the windows, the grounds showing thickly wooded. Time, the following day. Enter HYLAS *and* VOLINA.

VOLINA.

And have you come to see me ? 'tis too kind.
I cannot thank your highness, cannot reach
Up to your goodness' measure.   What tall terms
Could touch the top and pinnacle of your grace,
Which, to my loyalty's great obligation,
Has added that of saver of my life ?
So let me leave the labor of such load
Of thanks, high bearing to that eminence,
To Filippo, when grateful he returns ;
Till then, myself low lying at the base,
Up looking in mere mute acknowledgment.

HYLAS.

O, mind not that :—its mention yields us pain,
Whereof too much you yesterday endured ;
And which, alas ! has been the heavy price,
Paid by yourself, to purchase us the pleasure
Of your acquaintanceship in this retreat,
Sacred to you and mystic meditation.
How quiet is the quaint surrounding scene,
That seems a fair but slightly-frowning mistress
Tempting us from temptation of the town !
Such bowers might tempt a sybarite to come
And play therein the solemn anchorite.
I would I were a monk, to tread these shades,
Wherein you harbour and half-play the nun.

VOLINA.

Oh, fie ! a monk, and you about to marry ?

HYLAS.

I will not marry any ere I love.
We are indifferent toward this maid of Arno ;

Whose father's dukedom were a doubtful dower,
Should love not give true value to the treasure;
Without it, to my cold and vacant heart,
His child arriving as with empty hand.

VOLINA.

But she will bring love with her in her eyes.
As erst did men upspring of barren stones
Deucalion and Pyrrha cast behind them,
So, from the jetting of her glancing eyes,
Shall spring a score of sly, tormenting Cupids,
To plunge into your breast their tiny darts,
Whose points, alighting on your flinty heart,
Shall strike thence sparks to kindle the cold match
That will illume the lambent torch of Hymen.

HYLAS.

Teach me to woo her? I'll not have her else.

VOLINA.

She will compel you to prefer your suit;
Baptize you with love's fire, until you feel
The Pentecost of passion. Tongues shall sit
Upon you, till spontaneous eloquence,
Subdued, even by its own melodious voice,
(As the poor fabled snake self-stung to death,)
Swoons into sweeter silence.

HYLAS.

Be you not silent, 'tis so sweet to hear you.

VOLINA.

I've done.

HYLAS.

          Alas! too soon. Will Arno charm
Me thus? Come, teach me how to woo her.

VOLINA.

                                        Nay,
You are no novice, or are much belied.

HYLAS.

Yet we will fancy that our tongues are bells,
And you, of right, shall lead the merry peal,
Putting the all-unpractised chimes in tune,
That owe to be so blatant at my wedding.
Come, even Folly's voice is sometimes sweet,
And hoarse Despair doth oft make mellow music.
What, are your lips locked up ?—then I begin.
Mark, I now think you Arno, while you think
Me whomsoe'er you will : remember that.
First one salute, assuming your lips hers.   [*Salutes her.*

VOLINA (*rising*).

Oh, false assumption !   You must now begone :
I fear you are growing foolish, or else wicked.
Your highness must prune down audacity,
Or come no more to see me when alone.
Methinks that I had better banish you.
Should you return, your manners must be trimmed
Smooth as the shaven lawn or bordering box,
Or the clipped holly-edge of burnished green.
Nay, I am growing angry ; you must go,
Nor come again till comes back Filippo.

HYLAS.
Alas !

VOLINA.
        Begone, begone.

HYLAS.
                        Ah !

VOLINA.
                                You, about
To keep the marriage feast, should hallow you,
By keeping fast from ladies' lips ; at least
Should commerce hold with none except your love's,
Eschewing, as in Lent, forbidden flesh ;
Or merely begging others, as kind saints,
Add to your prayers for her their jaculate
" Amen."

D

HYLAS.

Would you walk veiled, or let those lids
Conceal your eyes, like nuns in marble cells,
Hither would I retire, perform my dues.
As ghostly father penance sets and shrives
Meek nuns, through Lent and austere Passion-week,
That they may keep unblameably glad Easter,
So, till my wedding-tide, would I come here,
That you might still confess and grave advise me.

VOLINA.

Yes, you would sin, that I might set you penance,
Still unperformed, in your afresh offending,
Yet for this first offence I must absolve you.
But no more say you know not how to woo :—
Forsooth, full fast you were just now a-learning!
You must begone ; this lesson is o'er long.

HYLAS.

And when return ?

VOLINA.

You shall be timed by me
In all your future visits to this house ;
As is the tide by the grave lady moon,
In its recurring progress to the shore.

HYLAS.

Then twice a day may I come hither, since
So often the indulgent moon allows
The tide come kissing up the wet-lipped sands.

VOLINA.

You turn my law to license. Fare you well.

HYLAS.

Farewell !—if must that word be said so soon.
Dare I ? [*making as though to re-salute her.*]
Farewell.   [*Exit.*

VOLINA.

Here am I, sun and moon,
And stars to steer by ; still abide at home,
And must receive the prince, should he return.

I am the moon, 'twould seem, to rule his tides.
Then flow, tides, toward the moon, and bathe this shore;
Yet flow not here too oft, lest some should say,
The moon is mad, or tide has lost its way.

[A voice heard singing without.

Who is lord of lordly fate,—
Lady of her lot's estate?
He who rules himself is he,
She who tempts not fate is she.

Who in peril stands of pain?
Who is sure to suffer stain?
He who climbs a thorny tree,
Gathers juicy berries she.

[A PAGE *enters and delivers a letter.*

VOLINA.

Who sings without?

PAGE.

A gypsy, that of late
To fill his own, comes read your servants' palms.
He haunts Gonardo's grounds e'en more than these.

VOLINA.

He sings not ill.—Behold the rooks come home;
And the low sun lies down amidst the trees.
Methinks 'twill rain, for rising is the breeze.

[Exit PAGE.

A letter from my lord.   His love not lags
Although himself grows old.   Would he were young
As Hylas!—Well, 'tis destiny, both whom
And when we wed.   Young men are indiscreet:
Old ones are wiser, though not quite so sweet;
While sweet is not, as mellow, such high praise,
And mellowness comes but from length of days.
The days are growing long, we growing tired.
The breeze still rises: be the casement closed.—

[Closing the casement.

Ah, while I dwell here cogitating, see,
Yonder Lord Hylas gazing on me free.

[Exit.

END OF THE SECOND ACT.

ACT III.

—

SCENE I.

A Hall of State in .Arno. DUKE OF ARNO, surrounded by its nobility. Before them, FILIPPO, SERAPHIO, PISANIO, MARCO, with the rest of FILIPPO's suite.

DUKE OF ARNO.

Peers of Pereza, excellent estates,
Sage seigniors, knights, courtly cavaliers,
Our gay-eyed guests, most gallant gentlemen,—
With all who here upon Pereza's part,
Compose and swell this welcome embassy,
That over our frontiers hath silken come
Waving its wooing way the wand of peace,
Your wont late in the light of glittering mail,
Dark-browed, to approach our scowling capital,
And in the hollow of this hall fling down
The gauntlet of defiance and of war;
Forgiving our unwillingest delay,
Now hear our answer homeward to your liege,
Our ancient and indomitable cousin,
Too long familiar to us but in feud,
To whom, and to his sole and loving son,
Along with you and our consenting court,
Thus 'tis our sovereign pleasure to reply:
So grave a butt and bound unto this arrow,
So marked and serious a proposition,
An issue so momentous as the wedding,
Not merely of two lovers, but two Dukedoms,
Caused our consideration and deep pause;
But which, being ended, we in brief declare:
Ta'en by report, that did forerun this suit,

With proffered picture of Pereza's son,
We do consent that here Lord Hylas come
To woo our daughter, who thereto agrees;
Ourselves concurring to bereave these arms,
So much do we admire the limned charms.

FILIPPO.

Thanks to your gracious highness for these words,
And double thanks unto your fair, frank daughter.
This to my sovereign and his suitor son,
I will, with happiest diligence, make known;
So, to that end, now, by your grace, take leave.

DUKE OF ARNO.

Now, fare you well, train of Perezan knights.
Commend us to the worthiest of your state.
Farewell, dear Count. Pray you, from us, present
This diamond to your lady,—token, tell her,
Of our esteem for you. Again farewell.
My lords of Arno, greet our parting friends.
Good seems begun; may it better ere it ends.

[*The* Duke, *having advanced and taken leave of* Filippo, *retires, gradually
followed by the nobility of Arno.*

FILIPPO (*aside*).

How will Volina joy when she beholds
This costly jewel, hearing me recite
The gracious words of flattery at its giving!
Now homeward to her, like a sunbeam quick.
Love grows in absence, as some plants in shade:
Fasting doth make it thrive. I will surprise her
By my despatch, outrunning expectation.
Grant my sick secretary mend, else love
Still fares upon thin thought.

PISANIO.

               Your excellency,
We prophesy, and dare now wager, that
The prince will plead his suit successfully.

FILIPPO.

Why not?

SERAPHIO.

He is averse to marriage, even
As too long was his father.

FILIPPO.

Let him hither,
And he must change his temper. This princess,
With golden glances and of mien divine,
This Ducal maid of Arno, might inspire
An emperor to the wooing of her charms.

SERAPHIO.

He is inspired by base Gallantio;
So moved by him, however we may strive
To bound and pale him in his proper park,
Will scarce refrain from shooting others' deer.

MARCO.

Why is that man not banished? Count, 'tis ill
To let him be at large.

FILIPPO.

The prince doth stand
Between us, that I cannot strike him down.
Yet will I do it, though not till be seen
Advantage; for, indeed, the wily villain,
Human in shape, in humour is a cross
'Twixt fox and wolf,—so subtle, bold, and savage.

SERAPHIO.

Too many a noble maid, and noble mother,
Bemoan his hungry and lascivious tooth.

MARCO.

He works his wickedness with secret charms.

FILIPPO.

Wherein they lie doth most astonish me,
Or whether of the person or the mind.

Coarse in his wit, mere carrion in form,
Wrecked in estate, forlorn in character ;
A cheat, a bully ; liar, lewd, profane ;
Rank in his life, and putrid in his soul ;
A ruffian that must ere now have rotted,
Were he not tinctured with the salt of courage.

PISANIO.

A monster formed, 'twould seem, to be abhorred.

MARCO.

A wretch that should be outlawed ; an assassin,
Casting his darts from out a hidden quiver.

SERAPHIO.

He is an Arab, wandering and wild,
That in Pereza, dreaded as disliked,
Lives like a roaming satyr, or abroad
Stalks o'er the dukedom, as of yore on earth,
Deserting Ida's and Olympus' crowns,
Wandered disguised, debauching Jupiter.

MARCO.

He, brazen, goes about equipped with bolts,
Watchful for woman's wounding.

PISANIO.

               And, alas !
Teaching to wield such, and still arming, Hylas,
Who boasts, himself, an armament of charms ;
Covered and compassed with them, even as
The porcupine with fabled missile quills.

FILIPPO.

He shall come hither and display his archery.—
Enough of this :—My lords, now let us go.
A word with you, my good Seraphio.

       [*Exeunt,* FILIPPO *conversing with* SERAPHIO.

SCENE II.

A Cabinet in the Ducal Palace at Pereza. DUKE *and* FIDEO.

DUKE (*with opened letters in his hand*).

Fideo, mine eyes, too weak, refuse to read
These papers. As an overburdened mule
Lies down i'the road, do they begin to swim;
So, as its master e'en takes off the load,
Do thou, I pray thee, take and read these letters.

FIDEO (*having received the letters*).

Two come from our love-embassy.

DUKE.
                                How long
Is it since it departed?—yesterday?
No, no; not all so recently. No, no,
It was not yesterday, but this day se'nnight.
Yet would it seem a year; still we could fancy
'Twere but an hour agone. Dear Fideo,
Inform us when our embassy left here:
Is it an hour, a week, or month, or year?

FIDEO.

Your highness dozes much, so loses reckoning
Of time's still adding figures, ever piling up
The columned moments; even as poor Crusoe
Lost the account on his notched calendar,
When, in the chase hurled o'er the precipice,
He, stunned, lay sleeping, nor e'er knew how long.
It is a fortnight now; but as a dream
Of minute's length will sometimes seem a year,
So doth this fortnight to your mind appear.

DUKE.

Ay, still the moments fall while we do sleep,
Piling our lives up, as in night heaps snow.
They might have been returned ere now.—Read, read.

FIDEO.

This from Count Filippo speaks of delay
To his return, from sickness in his train;
Likewise informs you of his full success,—
The prince invited to approach and woo.

DUKE.

Too good an issue for our sulking varlet!
Good Filippo, noble ambassador!—
Call Hylas hither. Worthiest Filippo!
Fideo, how fares his lady? Fair is she,
As he is noble. You have not forgot
How lovely, leaning on the grave count's arm,
She came, his bride, to our astonished court,
Dimming the lustre of its fair, fixed stars.
But she comes here no more, and all is night.—
Call Hylas hither.

FIDEO.

He is gone abroad.

DUKE.

With that pernicious one, Gallantio.

FIDEO.

Nay: he doth promenade alone of late.

DUKE.

'Tis good he shuns that minister of hell,
That ruiner of man's and woman's worth.
Deflowerer of all virtue, youths' path's pest,
His rank's reproach, a pander not a peer;
Who hath already, sore we grieve to say,
Made our son's youth, alas, familiar,
With creatures like himself, debauched and vile.
'Tis well, 'tis well: he shall to Arno straightway.—
Excellent Filippo! successful count!
Would he were here this instant. Fideo,
Your arm. Now are we grown a-weary sitting:

Read us the other missives in our room.
Allow us lean upon thee, Fideo:
A dying man requires a living staff.
Now let us travel.—What a little world
Is mine! the precincts of this palace: it
Not half explored; wings, corridors, stairs, aisles,
Vaults, garrets, offices, surrounding courts,
To me becoming as unknown, wild lands.
Lead me along; I totter toward the fall.
Now bear my body, presently my pall.

> [*Exeunt, the* DUKE *leaning on* FIDEO.

SCENE III.

—

An apartment in FILIPPO'S *mansion.* HYLAS *and* VOLINA.

VOLINA.

Nay, you are wittier, methinks, than wise.

> [*Enter a* PAGE *who presents a letter to* VOLINA.—*Exit* PAGE, *and*
> VOLINA *opens the letter.*]

Excuse me if I read: 'tis from my lord.

> [*Reads.*

HYLAS (*aside*).

Oh, that she were my lady! might those eyes
So brood and hover o'er a scrawl of mine!
She smiles, and, oh, it is as if the abyss
Had kindled, from the falling soft ajar
O' the coral gates of heaven; her lips heaven's gates,
Her teeth a little troop of ivory cherubs.
Again she smiles, again revealing them,
Whiter than Venus' yoke of drawing doves.
Oh, to be air to be indrawn between them,—
To be her breath to float into that heaven!
To be expelled indeed, but, with rich change,

To come forth incense.   Oh, to be a lamp,
To burn along with those bright eyes, for life,
On Hymen's altar !   Oh, hard fate ! hard fate !
Dark life that now must lie for ever waste,
Uncultivated, save by passion's plough !
Dash me to death, Fate, that has dashed fair life,
No more to be upbuilt on this rent base ;
But all its polished stones, at one discharge,
Scattered, as from the top of Etna, o'er life's lea ;
My cooled and quarried hopes around me lain,
Turned into pumice, lime-like rottenness.
Oh, Hylas, Hylas, what hast thou not missed,
In missing this fair creature !—Hist, she speaks.

VOLINA (re-folding the letter).

Your highness, even as I thought t'would prove,
In person must at Arno urge your suit.

HYLAS.

We have no suit at Arno.

VOLINA.

      You are grieved.
I pray your highness not to look so dull.
I've seen a miser who had just been robbed,
A lover lately jilted by his mistress,
But never have I seen one look so sad,
Who was so soon to be a buxom bridegroom.

HYLAS.

'Tis that which makes me sad.
Is it not wrong to marry me so young ?

VOLINA.

You urge me on to a dilemma's horns,—
You place me as between the fire and flood.
Should I say, yes, t'were to blame Filippo,
Condemn, and haply irritate, the Duke ;

Should I say, no, 'twould seem it would grieve you.
The case is delicate.

HYLAS.

Then let the delicate adjudge it: you
I constitute a court of high appeal;
Nor, till your verdict, will resign your hand.

VOLINA.

Oh, this is jest.

HYLAS.

Do I appear in jest?

VOLINA.

We'll think upon it. Pray release my hand.
Be I your court, we sit again to morrow,
When you may find your case in chancery.

HYLAS.

Let it remain there, so that I may come
Before you, pleading still my suit in person.

VOLINA.

But then might Filippo and the sovereign Duke
Come and dissolve the court, as all illegal.
Moreover, it were wrong to have a judge
Whom we have bribed. You bribed me recently,
More deeply than a mine of gold could do.
You know I owe you more than mere good-will.

HYLAS (aside).

Oh, that she owed me love! [aloud] What do you owe me?

VOLINA.

Oh, gratitude.

HYLAS.

And gratitude, methinks,
Brings with him, as accompanying sister, love;
Even as the true and vivid rainbow brings
Its sister-like reflection to the skies.

VOLINA.

You saved my life : what more could brother do ?

HYLAS.

Then you do love me even as a brother.
I love you too.

VOLINA.

   As you do love (and should love)
Each of your father's, and your future, subjects.

HYLAS.

So much that I could wish you were my princess.

VOLINA.

Fie ! Filippo hath found for you a princess.
Hath he not gone from here, as from the desert
Went Hebrew spies, and found you a rich land,
That doth await your going to possess it ?
He hath discovered you a golden fleece,
Expecting you its Jason. Oh, dismiss
That smile so bitter from your countenance,
That dims as Sol's when darkening in eclipse.
Why do you gaze so earnestly on mine,
As 'twere a sky and you astronomer ?
What see you on my face that so you con it,
As an astrologer his lying book ?
You can no more divine my thoughts, than I
Can yours.

HYLAS.

   Let us exchange our thoughts, as merchants
Exchange their wares, and so thereby grow rich ?
Ideas are as idle merchandise,
Of little value until trafficked with ;
And oft from dullest words, when bandied, spring
Most bright conceits, as out of base things start,
From their collision, sparks of rosy fire :
So tell me what you think.

VOLINA.

I were no woman
Did I.   Your father never yet demanded
His subjects' thoughts; though arbitrary, yet
Content with meaner, but more solid, tribute.
I will not, though your highness call me rebel.
Resign this hand.

HYLAS.

What ransom for the prisoner?

VOLINA.

It was not made a captive in fair war.
Be generous as the youthful Scipio
When he released the young Iberian maid.

HYLAS.

She was less fair than you, or he'd not done so.
[Kisses her hand passionately.

VOLINA.

Oh, you are fonder than we took you for!

HYLAS.

Oh, you are fairer than we yet have found!

VOLINA.

Begone: 'tis evening.

HYLAS.

I know it not;
So well the starlight of your eyes can feign,
The lustre of yon low, retiring sun.
It is not dusk where you are,—ever noon;
Your beauty dazzling more than doth yon sun;
Blinding me, that unseen is Arno's daughter,
And would be though she now before me stood,
With eyes self-lighting her so vaunted charms.

VOLINA.

You are the owl where you should be the eagle;
That is not blinded by the noontide sun,

No more than should be your young sovereign eye
By beauty, that should light you toward her sphere,
In willing thraldom of magnetic beams.

HYLAS.

We are enthralled by yours.

VOLINA.

Begone, begone.

HYLAS.

When you have broke my chains.

VOLINA.

You are not bound,
Not you.—Oh, shame on this! To Arno fly.

HYLAS.

It is not spring-time there, or else we might;
Playing, though pity, the untimeous swallow.

VOLINA.

Youth is the time to marry.

HYLAS.

True, for ladies.

VOLINA.

For gentlemen, knights, nobles, princes, all.

HYLAS.

My father married late, your lord at leisure.
We will not marry any ere we choose.

VOLINA.

Begone now, and think better of it: go.

HYLAS.

Recall that peevish mandate: 'tis too soon,
It is too harsh, to urge us from you thus.
Lo, where the sun yet peeps athwart the trees.

VOLINA.

It hath gone down, as you are charged to go.
Why would you linger ? you have lingered long.

HYLAS.

Who would not linger in a lady's eye ?
Who would not tarry on a lady's tongue ?
A little longer, longer would we linger,—
Yea, if we might, by the eternal gods,
Till night and weariness had sealed your lips ;
When we would stay, for you forbade it not.

VOLINA.

You are forbidden thus to raphsodize !—
Begged to avoid this strangely-charming ground.

[*Exit* HYLAS.

I now half wish that he had ne'er it found.
Truly, myself am growing melancholy.
What ail I with these faint conceits of folly ?

[*Exit.*

SCENE IV.

The Junction of GONARDO's *and* FILIPPO's *grounds. Time, immediately
after that of the last scene. Enter* GONARDO, *clothed in gypsy attire, with
his face and hands stained.*

GONARDO.

My lady deems I travel for my health.
So let her deem : I have not travelled far.
I have indeed of late been ill of doubt,
But shall not visit Hades ere my time,
Either for jaundice or for jealousy ;
Nor will continue to abide in Egypt,
Any longer have a skeleton at my feast,
Until I loathe the very dish I dip in.

[*Looking toward* FILIPPO's *mansion.*

Alas ! the prince hath found an entrance there.
Each day beholds him thither, as each day
Gallantio hovering here. To play the spy
Upon my neighbour scarcely suits my vein ;
But better hinder than wipe off a stain.

[*Exit.*

SCENE V.

Within GONARDO's *house.* PAPHIANA *and* GALLANTIO.

GALLANTIO.

Gonardo verging on his agony,
Tremohla trembling o'er the brink o'the grave,
Whereinto every day's more passing gust
Threatens to blow him, I shall soon, 'twould seem,
Be not alone thy true, acknowledged spouse,
But, at the Duke's death, Hylas' minister;
When all the large exchequer of the state
Shall be an ocean wherein I may dip
For us my thirsty hand.   Meantime, again,
Dear Paphiana, I beseech thee lend me
A hundred ducats.

PAPHIANA.

Give, not lend.   No, no,
I lend no more, thou most exorbitant man;
Nor would although thou wert a friar begging
For purposes of charity and pain,
As you still seek these largess but for pleasure.
Fond man, thou hast miscounted on me somewhat:
I have some yearning toward my husband now,
Who not alone of portion of his wealth,
But of his days by thee will have been robbed.
For shame, for shame, for shame, Gallantio!
Am I an oyster merely for your eating?
I see you simply use me for your purpose,—
Caress my hand that it may yield you gold.
You do not, nor did ever, mean to wed me.
Lend you another hundred ducats? shame!
I will not lend thee more.   Thou shalt repay
What I have lent, or, by Gonardo's ghost,—
Yes, by his ghost, for by this time he's dead,—

E

I will betake me crying to the Duke,
Yea, write myself unto Count Filippo,
Touching the prince's and thine own vile scheme
Against his honor.   I will publish thee,
Will paint thee over with mine own red wrongs,
That thou shalt seem more hell-hued than thou didst:
I will, as I myself am injured by thee,
And thou hast done thine utmost 'gainst Volina.
You be the prince's minister ?   Oh, folly,
That I should e'er have listened to such words !
Mark, I will write to Filippo at Arno,—
Bare your foul, mangled, cripple of a plot.

GALLANTIO.

Thou art the very keystone of its arch.

PAPHIANA.

Oh, thou arch-villain !—I your keystone ?
Then your whole devilry must fall to pieces:
I have withdrawn therefrom. Nefarious man,
What I have done, was it not at thy bidding ?

GALLANTIO.

What matters it who bade ? will that excuse thee ?
Canst thou at judgment cast thy sins on Satan,
And, lightened of them, saint-like, soar to heaven ?
No, thou art hung with us in the abyss,
O'er which we safely fly, unless, amidst,
Thou shear our wings in thy Parcaen mood.
Lend me a hundred ducats,—nay, no more.
Peace, peace, dove, wrath sets wrinkles in that front,
That varies as the hues of dying dolphin,
When it is lain upon the fatal deck.
Fie ! fatal flashes twinkle in thine eyes,
Thy bosom heaves now worse than rolling deck.
Oh, Paph, be soothed, forbid this hurricane ;
Come, let me coo away these dropping clouds,
That were not meant to variegate that brow,

As mingling colors pie the pigeon's neck.
Why shouldst thou paint that front? being **Paphiana**,
Why seekst thou to outpicture Iris?   Sweet,
Lend me the hundred ducats.—Dost thou keep
A clerk's account of all that thou dost lend me,
Since I will not repay thee else?   A hundred;
A hundred ducats for thy dear Gallantio.

PAPHIANA.

Where are the riches I've already lent you?

GALLANTIO.

Gone.

PAPHIANA.

Ay, gone: Gonardo's gone, or going! Thou
Extortioner, wretch, robber, plunderer,
Return the sums I have already lent thee.

GALLANTIO.

I will, I will, my silver Paphiana,
And give as interest my golden self.
Oh, let Gonardo go, for I am come,
And all that was of gone Gonardo good
Take from me,—yea, distil me till thou find
The golden grains and essence of a man
In thine esteem's alembic.

PAPHIANA.

                    Thou vile sponge,
Speak not Gonardo's name; but give me back
Gonardo's ducats that my hand hath passed
To thine, as into bushel without bottom.
Where are his ducats, rogue? where are the ducats?

GALLANTIO.

Even where another hundred, Paph, shall find,
And bring them back, the wandering prodigals.
This hundred, hark, is but to mend a net,
Wherein I'll take thee more than thou hast lost,—

Mere bait for hook, with which I'll take what I
Half fear to tell thee, such a golden gudgeon.

PAPHIANA.

I am no more your gudgeon.

GALLANTIO.

But thou art.
Whose else art thou, my plump one ?   Twenty like thee
Would sink the smack of Zebedee's two sons.

PAPHIANA.

Would thou wert drowned !

GALLANTIO.

I'the sea of Gallilee ?

PAPHIANA.

I'd weep my very eyes out, sir, to drown ye,

GALLANTIO.

Oh, keep thine eyes for better purposes.
Pray lend me some small bait, that I, therewith,
May take for thee a most miraculous draught.
Lend me those ducats.

PAPHIANA.

I will lend no more.

GALLANTIO.

I pray you do.

PAPHIANA.

I will not.

GALLANTIO.

No ?

PAPHIANA.

Not I.

GALLANTIO.

I know thou wilt.

PAPHIANA.

Do you ? indeed you lie.

GALLANTIO.

Yes, oft by thee.

PAPHIANA.

But never more: I've said it.

GALLANTIO.

I would believe thee if thou wert not woman.

PAPHIANA.

You are no man to taunt thuswise a woman.

GALLANTIO.

You are no woman thus to stint a man.

PAPHIANA.

I will not lend you more, howe'er you sue.
Borrow of Hylas.

GALLANTIO.

As yon sky is now
Without a cloud, so now is Hylas' purse
Without a ducat.—Nay, I now confess
(Which I before did not intend to do)
I wish to borrow but to lend to Hylas,
Who is already a mine deep my debtor,
And hath engaged, that, at his soon accession,
He will reimburse me in rich sinecures;
Giving compensation, from the public purse,
For all my many secret services.
Lend me the dirty ducats.

PAPHIANA.

Say that you
Will ask of me no more till we are wed.

GALLANTIO.

But what if Hylas should again entreat me,
Holding thee in reversion for a countess?
When with a title thou mayest flout Volina.
Give me the hundred ducats.   This is sure,
That when the Duke is dead, which must be soon,

I shall be rich as Crœsus; for estate,
Having the state, that, though the Prince be Duke,
Shall be my fief, whereon to build a gallows
To hang the fools who counselled my proscription.
Dearest, those ducats;—say two hundred, love.

PAPHIANA (*giving the ducats*).

Take them.   They are Gonardo's, if he lives:
But I believe he has been dead some days;
For I have seen a creature like his ghost
Prowling about these doors,—and yet so dark
A thing, it were to count my husband lost
To deem I had in earnest seen his shade.

GALLANTIO.

When he is dead, they'll keep his shade in heaven.
Are here two hundred?—Whereat gaze you now?

PAPHIANA.

The very form I spoke of has passed by!

GALLANTIO.

Pshaw! mind it not, nor ponder on thy spouse:
Nor grieve that I so soon must fly away;
For I must leave thee for the fledgling Hylas,
Who now expects me, and of late hath lived
On expectation, growing pale upon it,
As one who sickens into a decline.

PAPHIANA.

What favor finds he with the fair Volina?

GALLANTIO.

Volina, wanton, holds him off and on;
Playing, with the light gusts of her vagrant breath,
Around his purpose, filling not its sails;
While he, afraid to row into her haven,
(Or heaven rather,) out in the rough offing,
Where swells and flows his longing's vexèd tides,

Tosses and rolls until he leaks out tears,
And chides the surge when he believes none hears.

PAPHIANA.

Mark, this young boar of old Count Filippo's woods
Must quickly find his medicinal root,
Or die (if men indeed e'er die of love):
The Count's return must be expected daily.

GALLANTIO.

Fear not: he comes not yet.—At once, good bye.   [*Exit.*

PAPHIANA.

Why have I chosen yonder wasteful man?
Why quake so at a swarthy beggar's sight?
Oh, conscience, thou hast taken away my courage!
What have I done? what shall I do?   Would I
Could undo what is done!   Away, such thoughts!
Life flies away with all toward death.   Perchance
This hour the wronged Gonardo lieth dead;—
Yet evil hour in which I wronged Gonardo!
In evil day I knew Gallantio!
But let Gonardo die,—even let Gonardo
Die; for I then shall injure him no more,
'Gainst him augmenting not my sin's old score.
How swift a score Gallantio hath made!
Oh, woman, grant to man what he doth crave,
For ever after thou art his poor slave.   [*Exit.*

END OF THE THIRD ACT.

ACT IV.

———

SCENE I.

Within the Ducal palace at Arno. FILIPPO *and* SERAPHIO.

FILIPPO.

This sudden sickness of our secretary
Is most untoward, for I will not leave him.

SERAPHIO.

He hath strange symptoms: not like those that oft
Do visit strangers on their coming hither;
But such a full prostration of his strength,
'Twould seem one might presume to count his hours.

FILIPPO.

'Tis a sharp fit; but youth's the champion
Fights best with death, or were we more alarmed.
The worst, we trust, will be some days' delay.
We prize him, and, our errand being sped,
Desire forthwith to swiftly journey home.
          [*Enter a* PAGE, *who gives* FILIPPO *a letter.—Exit* PAGE.
Aside] It is not from Volina.   It is strange,
Most strange, she writes not.   Haply she forbears,
Expecting my return still day by day.
                    [*Reading the letter.*

When the sun's on the cask, the wine turneth sour;
While the rain stays in heaven, on earth fades the flower;
While the man is at market, the maiden will cheat him;
Ripe peaches, exposed, prompt sparrows to eat 'em;
The red, blooming cherry, o'erweathered, is found
To blacken and wither, and fall to the ground;

The brightest of swords in the dew will corrode;
Beneath the rich strawberry crouches the toad;
When pears are in season, of medlars beware:
Return, Filippo, and look after your mare.

What means this strange epistle? Be I right,
Its purport seems all hinting at some hazard
Frowning on me or mine. What hazard? Surely
All's well at home; but much my heart misgives me.

       [Having re-read the letter.

A sting is in its tail! a scorpion's too.—
Who sends this barbèd shaft? it saith not who.

    SERAPHIO.

I fear your letter doth contain ill news.
I hope the Duke bears up; no wilder Hylas.

    FILIPPO.

I hope so too; but on that score naught saith it.

    SERAPHIO.

I trust no private cause for your annoyance.—
Forgive me asking you.

    FILIPPO (*aside*).

     I'll burn it!—No:
Seraphio is shrewd; he shall peruse it.
Aloud.] 'Tis somewhat private, but, Seraphio,
You are my friend, have known me from my youth,
Danced at my wedding, and (what God's denied)
Would have become the sponsor to my child,
Had Heaven sent me one.—Read this, then say,
If a truth-teller thou believ'st hath sent it.

   SERAPHIO (*after having read the letter*).

'Tis all truth in the letter; yet may be,
In spirit, merely a malicious lie.

    FILIPPO.

Expose your thoughts, give fear unfeigned expression;
For that you fear, I gather from your caution:
There must be mire, when people pick their way.

SERAPHIO.

Trouble not yourself concerning this strange letter,
That shews not full and finishing hand of truth,
But only stump of fearful-fingered fraud;
As if the hand had once been in a trap,
From which, as rats will gnaw off their own limbs,
It had escaped but by self-amputation.
It lacketh signature, nor doth it bear
One well-cut feature of faced circumstance;
But merely daubs in some proverbial truths,
Meaning that you shall fancy and compose them
Into a countenance of false conclusions.

FILIPPO.

Do you so think?

SERAPHIO.

I do.   Let me advise
You to contemn, as I, the rhymed enigma.
I see you are troubled still.

FILIPPO.

Yes, somewhat, somewhat.

SERAPHIO.

Be pacified, my lord.

FILIPPO.

Seraphio,
Two nights agone, I had an evil dream.
Methought I saw Volina sore beset;
And when I did approach to rescue her,
She, weeping, turned away, and, at my feet,
Sunk into darkness.

SERAPHIO.

'Twas an ugly dream.

FILIPPO.

'T seems uglier now.

SERAPHIO.

But as for dreams,
What are they?—and, indeed, what are they not?

They are fantastic vapors of the brain,
Wreathing round slumber's pillow,—shapes of thought,
Appearing on the half-extinguished soul,
As forms of creatures on expiring embers.

FILIPPO.

The dream and letter countenance each other.

SERAPHIO.

Somewhat they do.

FILIPPO.

I know not what to think.

SERAPHIO.

Neither do I.

FILIPPO.

Can it be possible
That, in the envisioned hour, our guardian angel
May sometimes to the soul's unmoving eyes,
Hold, as it were, a clear Pygmalion mirror,
Wherein she sees the then enacting deed?
This written disc lacks not its pointing gnomon;
Though all's so shadowy that I cannot tell
The hour, for want of sun upon the dial.
Like me, you stand perplexed.

SERAPHIO.

I could myself,
Now count this dark and inky sketch as having,
Or having not, verisimilitude.—
'Tis as the soapy bubbles children blow,
That, floating in the light, take various hues.
But think no more on't.

FILIPPO.

'Twill not be so served.
This letter does not lie, however falsely
It may interpret darkly-seeming shows.

SERAPHIO.

Then, for your satisfaction, by your leave,
I for Pereza will forthwith take horse;

And there,—while it believes me still in Arno,—
Disguised, discern if aught can be amiss.

FILIPPO.

Go, good Seraphio; invisibly
As 'twere: but let no rustling of thy vestments
Alarm my lady. Do not play the wasp,
But act the harmless, though industrious, bee;—
Yet even he must all suppress his hum.
Away, dear friend.

SERAPHIO.

I will at once depart. [*Exit.*

FILIPPO.

Is there some mystic and invisible bond
That ever links us unto those we love?
Or doth love's strong and melting power transfuse
Two souls until they do compose but one?
I fear not for Volina: wherefore should I?
Did never doubt her,—never had occasion;
While a discreeter agent none could use
Than is Seraphio.
Should evil now be meant me,
Seraphio will learn it. He shall go,—
Though nothing he'll discover, save his friend
Too fond! What impious Perezan Titan
Would pile his passage to my lonely star;
Or, having dared approach her glorious sphere,
Is not already by her frown thence hurled,
As Satan from the living light of heaven?
Heaven's living light shall gild this world no more,
When she doth cease to love me as she swore. [*Exit.*

SCENE II.

A Corridor in the Ducal Palace at Pereza. Moonlight.

GALLANTIO (*folding a letter*).

So, from these tidings, all at Arno's well,
Seeing the secretary lies so ill.

The master yet must sicken,—not of poison,
But of despair, the devil's malady.
His potion shall be Hylas, whom we see
Yonder, here coming to bemoan himself,
Looking disconsolate as that fallen angel:
So put a mask of melancholy on,
That we, too, seeming of the serious sort,
May be admitted to his sorrow's rites.

[GALLANTIO *paces to and fro with a gloomy air: at length* HYLAS, *having perceived, approaches him.*

HYLAS.

Wherefore do you appear so dull to-night?

GALLANTIO.

Is it your highness? Pray forgive me, but
Gonardo sickens faster than I wish him.
Letters, as thick as snow-flakes from the north,
Come from Turin declaring him near death.

HYLAS.

Doth that chagrin you?

GALLANTIO.

     And enough. The fool!
Who, spurred by jealousy, fast towards his end,
Gallops, bestridden by the rider, sickness;
That soon will force him, with the whip of pain,
Across death's dark and dismal ditch, to leap
Or to the pit of hell or field of heaven.—
Heaven take Gonardo's widow! Should he die,
I will not wed her, though each day I swear it.

HYLAS.

Would Filippo were sick! then he might die
And leave his wife a widow.

GALLANTIO.

     Life is swift
And swifter the brief spring-tide of the blood.
Would you, awaiting Filippo's demise,

Stand as the Roman rustic on the bank,
Waiting the total rushing by of Rhone?
As rapid rivers wear away their banks,
So moving moments steal the bloom from woman.—
Embark while plays the wind upon your sails.

HYLAS.

This were too foul a play on Filippo.

GALLANTIO.

Let him not see it, 'tis nor foul nor fair.
To him that sleepeth, what imports the weather?
The absent are unconscious as the dead.

HYLAS.

Gallantio, we cannot harm his lady,—
Will not so wrong her, and, with her, her lord.

GALLANTIO.

Had I your place, your person, and your parts,
I'd right myself, yet do no wrong to either.

HYLAS.

Nay, if we thought we could so please our sense,
Could hug such bliss transcendent to our soul,
And Filippo no wiser be nor wretched,—

GALLANTIO.

Who sees nought, hears nought, feels nought, grows not wiser;
No wiser growing, grows not wretched. Listen:
When she doth serve a beggar at her gate,
What poorer is her husband? and if she
Should give you crumbs of kisses day by day,
What meaner were the master's evening feast?
Though she should cram the wallet of your wish,
It would not lessen Filippo's rich store.

HYLAS.

But, oh! how poor would it not leave herself,
Who, with those crumbs, must give me all her honor;

Yea, all in want and utter nakedness,
Henceforward stand before my prurient gaze.

GALLANTIO.

Fig-leaves will cover all 'twixt her and you;
While secresy's impenetrable robe
Conceals her from her husband and the world.

HYLAS.

When Eve had tasted of the tree of knowledge,
The flaming cherubs drove her to the world;—
And she is innocent as ere was Eve.

GALLANTIO.

Your innocence is but a doll for maids.
Her airs are merely feints to eager you;
Her dalliance, a spur to make you speed.

HYLAS.

In vain you meet me with these apt replies:
I shall not see again the fair enchantress.

GALLANTIO.

See her this very night. Delay makes sick:—
Lo! the lean wolf of unfulfilled desire
Lairs on your hollowing cheek. Be resolute.

HYLAS.

What matters resolution? in her presence
The angel love pleads down the devil lust.
Each day beholds me conquered, who went forth
Meaning that day to conquer; sees me hence
Departing hot as fire-filled chafing-dish,
Returning chill as it when void of coals;
Views an Iconoclast that, at the shrine,
Still bows to image he's approached to break.
Urge us no more to evil; we'll not hear on't;
For we should fear our soul were banned from heaven
Did we accomplish now your full desire.
Good night to you:—too long we stay, we fear,
To interrupt your meditations here.
                                                    [*Exit.*

GALLANTIO.

His thick desire hath cleared itself to love;
And love is ever a contrary ass,
That goading only brings unto a stand.
What new expedient?—Love, come; lust, go:
With either I will yet wound Filippo.   [*Exit.*

SCENE III.

—

A Library within the Ducal Palace at Arno.

FILIPPO (*sitting with books before him*).

Quiet thee, heart: it is too soon, too soon
To dream of swift Seraphio's return.
                    [*Enter* SERAPHIO *in a riding-habit all soiled.*
Seraphio!
Oh, friend, your name this instant left my lips,
Thence flying forth into the ocean air,
Through which you've cut your passage as the dove
That beareth perfumed missives 'neath its wings.
How is my lady? say, how fares my wife?

SERAPHIO.

Well; therefore you may set your mind at ease.

FILIPPO.

'Tis easier: yet in these volumes no
Still nook of dun abstraction have I found,
Though sedulously sought; but, in the stead
Thereof, a throng of sore presentiments,
Since you departed, at the thought of her,
Have thick beset me; as do flies beset
Him who doth take i' the sun his noon-day meal.
But are you sure no trouble threats Volina?
Hath nothing menaced, nothing trivial
Annoyed her? not a gust, a shower, a breath?

SERAPHIO.

Nought have I found, though I have sought as closely
As my unwarranted hand, (being, as you know,
And even at your own injunction too,)
Gloved in a secret quest and stiff disguise,
Could, without brushing off the dewy quiet,
That still hath lain upon your scented flower.
Had I done more ere dawn of your return,
Her petals might have opened in suspicion
At the unwonted touch, to close no more;
Or, should they have re-slept upon their stalk,
Had dreams, to her as painful as to you
The dream you sent me from you to resolve.

FILIPPO.

'Twas prudent; you have acted warily,
As I expected:—but, Seraphio,
None e'er had riches and not feared the thief.

SERAPHIO.

Your lady is her own best key and coffer.

FILIPPO.

Nay, who shall doubt it? so is each true wife.
I shame to think on 't,—but that dream, that letter:—
Not that I did mistrust Volina; pshaw!
Mistrusts the earth the sun on cloudy days?
Becomes she jealous of the moon and stars
When fogs conceal them from her in November?
But thus I thought: now in my absence' night;
Amidst the room and quiet of my home,
Her beauty, shining as a full-orbed lamp,
Attracts the moth.   Thus much I feared; no more.
Dost think we'd play the elderly-wed fool,
Doubting his wife because she is his younger?
The younger toward the elder still inclines,
As youthful flowers toward the antique sun;
While maids despise, or shyly turn away,
With angry blushes, their regards from youths,

F

Or drop their veiling lids, as eve's flowers fold
And plait their petals o'er their heads, to shun
The cold and saucy gazes of the stars.

SERAPHIO.

For that your warrant were your lady's love,
And plighted, true affection.

FILIPPO.

Even so.

Oh, wretchedest of wretches is the man,
Caught in the whirlpool, jealousy! not fly,
Caught in the borders of the spider's web,
Faster entangled; spider not so cruel,
Returning still to sting the fettered fly,
As the recurring thought of wife untrue.

SERAPHIO.

Your dream and letter were two gusts to puff you
Against the meshes wherein sits the monster,
Out of whose snares whoso escapes alive
Goes ever after sickly and unsound,
Prone to relapse at each suspicious cloud,
And cold east wind of sudden nipping doubt;
Even as one whose youth some fearful fit
Of trembling ague shook and undermined.
Pray, mind your health henceforth.—How's Plumio's?

FILIPPO.

Worse.

I cannot, will not, leave him till he dies,
Or it be seen he shall not die, but live.

SERAPHIO.

Poor youth! so faithful he has been to you.

FILIPPO.

I never found him in a wilful fault.
Visit him when you may have rested you,
And see how likely looks he for the tomb.

SERAPHIO.

We'll with you there to rest us in his room.

[*Exeunt.*

SCENE IV.

A Room in FILIPPO'S *Mansion.*

VOLINA (*entering*).

How dim the house appears! how woe-begone!
How evening-like at noon, in May, November;
Day's flambeau dwindled into taper twilight,
The light gone out that recently illumed!
How every blind seems closed for death and dole!
A hazy curtain seems to cover all,
A foggy film t' afflict these wandering eyes,
That rove as over vaguest images;
As invalid's upon the couch by night,
Darkling, descry imaginary forms;
Or his, that, being dazzled by the sun,
Distinguish nothing but false, floating hues.
Oh, Hylas, thou hast dazzled these weak eyes,
That they see nothing, or see only thee!

[*Enter a* PAGE.

PAGE.

My lady, please you, the Lord Hylas comes.

[*Enter* HYLAS *and exit* PAGE.

VOLINA.

I must be stern; indeed, must now be angry.
Your highness was requested to refrain,
Yea, charged that until Filippo's return
You would not pay me any further visits.

HYLAS.

Charge me to chain myself unto a rock,
Or lock myself in a dark vaulted cell,
And, through the grating, throw away the key
Into the neighbouring, unrestoring tide;
For that were easier than to restrain
Myself from your dear presence while I'm free.

VOLINA.

Alas, alas! oh, straight your highness hence:
Oh, pardon me confirming still my hest!
You must no longer come to see me thus.

HYLAS.

Take me into your service in disguise.
I'll be your page, your footman, what you choose,
So I be near to look upon and love you.

VOLINA.

Away; and cease such unbecoming words.
Why hath your highness put me to this test?
You rave:—oh, do not gaze so on my face;
These charms of mine will fade, and, even though
They had obtained a life-long lease of bloom,
Must be my husband's till they find the tomb.

HYLAS.

No! for a while, I swear, they shall be mine:
Too much for one proprietor those charms.
Shall one man's eye attempt to assume the sun,
Leaving the world in gloom?

VOLINA.

              Oh, veil your eyes,
That glare a hideous comment on your words;
Turn, turn away your gaze.

HYLAS.

Why were you made so fair?

VOLINA.

Ask Heaven, if you do think me so.

HYLAS.

For the same reason that the rose is fair.—
Oh, you are far too fair to bloom in shade,
Too fair to be forsaken!

VOLINA.

Oh, your highness, hence.
Cause not my cheek consume itself with shame.
There is grave guilt in longer hearing you.

HYLAS.

Is it a crime to love you ?

VOLINA.

Yes, high treason ;
(And who should hate that crime so much as you ?)
Treason against my husband.

HYLAS.

When returns he ?

VOLINA.

I know not : why ?

HYLAS.

That I may know the days I have to live ;
For Filippo's return is my last hour.

VOLINA.

You will not kill yourself ?

HYLAS.

No : like a sprite,
Whose body lies unburied, unembalmed,
Henceforward only wander in the world,
Till death (should we unhappily survive you)
Inform us that we may at last take rest,
Going with you into Elysium.

VOLINA.

Ah, would that we had never met on earth !
Hylas, away ; oh, hence !

HYLAS.

Farewell, farewell.
Earth from this hour to Hylas is but hell.

[*Rushes out.*

VOLINA.

Now, you conjugal Powers that hover here,
Ye jealous wardens of our constancy,
That reaches to the thought, assist me ! now,
Out of my bosom, thou mock chastity,
Or make me virtuous all.   Oh, God ! oh, Christ !

Thou that in pity look'd'st on Magdalen,
Nor didst rebuke her when she washed thy feet,
Rebuke not me, but tell me,—gracious tell me,
Is pity shewn to Hylas criminal?
Do not the guiltless angels love each other?
Oh, Hylas, Hylas, hadst thou been my brother,
We might have loved each other without blame,
But now the thought on't crimsons me with shame.   [*Exit.*

SCENE V.

Within the Palace at Arno.   Two COURTIERS.   *A sound of distant music.
Time, evening.*

FIRST COURTIER.

Hylas is absent from the revelry.

SECOND COURTIER.

My lord, my lord, the prince is changed of late;
To every eye appears to waste and pine:
'Tis said from sheer vexation at this marriage.

FIRST COURTIER.

Assuredly he grieves and chafes at something;
Walks sadly to and fro; oft, with a frown,
Hies forth, as if on desperate purpose bent;
And, strange and ominous, pays daily visits
To Filippo's fair lady,—as some say,
To beg her intercession with her lord,
To save him now from wedlock.

SECOND COURTIER.

                    Dangerous suit!
Have you not heard th' injurious report?

FIRST COURTIER.

I have, dear sir; but careful how you speak.
Lend not a feather of your breath to help

To plume the flying scandal; since report,
Even when good, is often merely—what?
Zephyrus playing on Eölian harp;
While here its whisper, sinistrous as its mien,
More dismal than the thaw-wind comes,—yea, hoarser
Than we have yet heard slander's blackest wings.

SECOND COURTIER.

I shall herein keep silence, my good lord.—
But see where Hylas and Gallantio come.
They seem to be at odds, too long too even.
Let us retire: the prince appears displeased,
Chiding, methinks, yonder opprobrious peer.

[Exeunt, and enter HYLAS and GALLANTIO.

GALLANTIO.

Ay, ay, abandon her,—confess you foiled.
What matters it to me that you be foiled?
Threaten; make now of me your rude fist's foil.
Thrust, thrust: I shall not parry. Slay me now.
Vent your vexation: I will not reply.
Shed showers of epithets upon these shoulders,
That late have worn the world's san-benito
That yours might yet be flaunted ivory bare.
Keep bared your tongue; abuse me: you are licensed.
Vomit your vengeance on this offered head.
Spit spitefully in this face; spit at my breast
Ungrateful venom till it reach my heart.
Banish me, if you choose: I am your slave,
Your scapegoat. Drive me to the wilderness.
Curse me; empty your anger's magazine.
Pour on, bombard.

HYLAS.

      Imprecate not too much,
Or we may grant thy prayers. Why hast thou urged,
Wherefore inspired, us to attempt and seize
The fairest citadel in Italy?

GALLANTIO.

Again take your artillery to the breach.

HYLAS.

Take thy now odious counsel down to hell,
Whereto thy courses lead thee.   Traitor, hence!

GALLANTIO.

I am no traitor towards your highness: no,
But ever loyal, diligent, and true;
Disinterested, and most so in this.

HYLAS.

Revenge, revenge, revenge on Filippo!
Base peer, what carest thou for my delight?
Thou hatest Filippo, I know thou dost,
And wouldst herein have made of me thy tool;
But hast most falsely reckoned on our temper.
By heaven, sirrah! say, shall we become
A mere cat's-paw, so you can snatch, unharmed,
Your nuts from hot retaliation's fire?
Or do you deem us even so besotted,
We cannot tell your black, intruded palm,
From ministering angel's white and gentle hand?

GALLANTIO.

Your highness cannot tell a friend from foe
Now, being drunken with love's heady wine;
But as a toper homeward bound i'the dark,
Having missed his door, stumbles bewildered on,
And, wildly groping, clutches every latch,
So now your highness wildly clutches me;
And as that silly toper, having forced,
At last, his way into another's house,
And therein finding lonely, watching woman,
For his own wife mistaken, falls to scold her,
Because the cottage wears an altered face,
Even so do you, in your mistaking mood,
Unreasonably call me to account,
Because your amour is not prosperous.

HYLAS.

Ah, how thou wouldst persuade me thou art white,
Although I see thee of the negro dip!
Why is thy skin so fair?   Buy thee a vat,
And dye, or damn thee, black as Lucifer.
Do we not know thou hatest Filippo?

GALLANTIO.

Do we not know you love his lady?   Go
Once more to visit her, and with you take
This purse, and of its solid parts compose
A pick-lock to Volina's bolted charms.
One told me, but to-day, the road is dropped
With gold, that leads unto my lady's shrine.
Frown not, I tell you what myself was told.—
There's meaning in Danaë's shower of gold.

HYLAS.

Now know we not or to abhor or love thee!
By heaven, were we sure thou coin'st a lie,
Thou with those coins shouldst have dashed out thy brains.
Afford us proof, (for all depends on this,)
That we may settle whether to pursue
This roe, thou swearest is already struck,
Or turn upon our track and strike down thee.
Bring the impugner of her honor hither.

GALLANTIO.

Honor in man is sacred as in woman;
Nor should the reputation of the latter,
With proud hoof, be allowed to override
The former's humbler steed, veracity.
I am not bound in honor to divulge,
But to retain, what was in honor told.

HYLAS.

This shall be seen to: bring him.

GALLANTIO.

                    It would seem
You would not see it though I brought the sun,

And held it as a candle in my hand,
Whereby to con this scrawl on scandal's page.

HYLAS.

We'll know the truth of what thou hast averred.

GALLANTIO.

Travel by the same gilded chariot
As others have done and you shall.

HYLAS.

Oh, thou that deem'st the world a sordid show!
Oh, gilded falsehood! basest lie of brass!
Thou brazen brow, thou cruel, cool defamer,
Doth not thy heart grow molten with remorse,
And coin itself away in yellow drops,
To compensate this lady for aught lost
By forgery from thy malicious brain?
But know, thou utterer of slander's coin,
(Thyself so base grown, that thy sterling peers
Esteem thee counterfeit,) that thou art now
Nailed to the counter; likewise be assured,
It were thy last, as well as greatest, crime,
To circulate this fiction past belief.

GALLANTIO.

Believe it, or believe it not, no matter:
Style me, or not, arch-heretic, because
I do not count your saint immaculate;
To preach which doctrine doth appear a crime:—
Farewell, I lose my temper and my time.   [*Exit.*

HYLAS.

Too gross an actor he upon life's stage,
Rehearse aright a speech of true-love passion.
He deems all men are false, all women lewd.
Audacious liar, most mistaken villain!

[*Exit, and enter a* LADY *of the Court.*

LADY.

What noise was that, as if of quarrelling?
It seemed Lord Hylas' voice, erratic rising
From ground of grief to cloud of indignation.

Forlornest bird! once caught so easily,
Now hopping from me still from twig to twig,
Its backward eyes informed with angry care;—
Grown all unsocial, ungregarious;
Shy as the wagtail, solemn as the owl,
Who, ere this threatened wedding's wintry flaw,
Was lively as the linnet in the spring.
'Twould take a bevy now of lady-birds
To catch my lately lightsome caroller.
Where doth the ostrich hide its head?   How shall I
Besprinkle salt on the spry sparrow's tail?
I have seen boys place grain beneath a riddle,
To which they had attached a cord, that, pulled,
Down tumbles riddle, underneath quakes bird.
I would I had him underneath my riddle!
Big though he be, and churlish grown as Orson,
He must be soon within my custody;
Accompany me, who am appointed marshal
To apprehend and bring him to the Duke.

        [*Exit, and presently re-enter* HYLAS.

        HYLAS.

No rest, no rest for my afflicted foot,
Thrust (not by my Noachic sire, but rudely)
Out of the ark by yon accursed Ham.
Whence came that wealth? 'tis said he ever hangs,
Not only on the gibbet o'the world's scorn,
But o'er the gulf of yawning destitution.
He wins at play, with his intrigues repairs
The rope that still suspends him over Hinnom.
Let him therewith buy masses for his soul,
Be it not (as much we fear) past praying for.
We will consort with one so vile no longer;
Strong once our liking, now our loathing stronger.
Ah me!   [*The cawing of a rook heard without.*
It is the black, belated rook's harsh cry.
Hie thee, bird, howeward to thy dusky holt,
For there Volina is.   Thou knowest not grief,
Though crabbed thy voice, nor omen bring'st of ill

Like that which now we bear.   Our note is changed,
Not thine: that as to-day will sound to-morrow.
None but man sings to satisfy his sorrow.
I'll try to overtake thee with my words,
And drown the sound of yonder growing mirth.

[*Sings.*

Croaking raven, sailing by,
Bird that homeward sullen swings,
Waft me sullen through the sky,
Sullen thoughts of sable dye,
Sable as thy sullen wings.

II.

Truant from Volina's woods,
Words for fair Volina dear,
Sweep the intervening roods,
Tell Volina Hylas broods
Sorrowful and sighing here.

III.

Tell her, though the amorous fair,
Partnered, make new day of night,
Though their lute-lips fill the air
With music, Hylas, in despair,
Seems in but a haunted night.

IV.

Tell Volina, vagrant bird,
Hylas in his hollow room,
Brooding, utters not a word;
Dumb and doleful broods unheard,
Like sad spirit in a tomb.

[*Re-enter the* LADY *of the Court.*

LADY.

Still on the melancholy minor?   Oh,
The Duke your father loved a merrier key
When he was your years:—he enquires for you.
Cease moping here, and come along with me:
Your highness needs a keeper.—Will you come?

HYLAS.

Ah, madam, is it you?

LADY.

You know me not?

HYLAS.

In truth I did not, you have grown so fair.—
Is it with rolling in the dew?

LADY.

Oh, shame!

HYLAS.

Forgive us: we have grown barbarian.—
But you have ceased to paint.

LADY.

How know you that?

HYLAS.

I can approve it by those tints being fast.
Lately we cease salute the ladies, but—   [*Salutes her.*
Your cheek wears nature's colors.

LADY.

Yes, and you,
With mordant of your lips, would bite them in.
Fie! you have grown no better than you were.

HYLAS.

I love to see you wrath; for then your eyes
Fling fire like two divine incendiaries.
Lend me your hands, those ministers of mischief.
Ah [*sighing*], once, my lady, when we took them thus,
These fingers were ten waxen torches, kindling
Love's bonfire.

LADY.

Oh, such sighs as these
Would puff out Cupid's.

HYLAS.

You are Iris; your
Bedizzened hands show like dove's changeful necks.
Methinks that these are jewels:—are you wed?

LADY.

Have you forgotten?

HYLAS.

Nigh forgot myself!
And yet you are the same you ever were:—
But little charm you now.   Go, get you gone.

LADY.

Will you go with me?

HYLAS.

No, I will not.—Still
You go not, madam;—stay, then, and observe.—
But mark with modest eyes my naked grief.
Oh, how you eye me, madam Momus;—yet
I love your eyes, for them you cannot paint;
No more than Titian could have stained the sky.
All over else you are deceivers; there
You are yourselves.

LADY.

Oh, libellous lips! now mine
Shall not retain that false salute from yours.

HYLAS.

Return it, meek one.

LADY.

It is worthless now;
So even let it hang upon my lips,
As we in hall see paper roses hang,
At Christmas on the gathered evergreen.
Who smells at those?   You yet have many left
For whom you choose.   Red roses grow again
On the same bush whence roses have been culled.
Some ladies' lips more honey yield more gathered,
As ruddy kine more milk more they be drained.

HYLAS.

Whose lips taught you such lore?   Read you by touch,
As do the blind?   Ourselves have well-nigh ceased
Poring o'er ladies' vermeil-vellum cheeks.
Believe us,—but we know you now will laugh,—
Ourselves are but a poor spoiled paragraph.

LADY.

'Twere hard to laugh at a confronting truth.

HYLAS.

The world's a book, and men and women pages.

LADY.

Oh, you are hypochondriacal, full
Of gloomy gall.

HYLAS.

     We have been taking bitters.

LADY.

Your highness grows too tart.

HYLAS.

         Forgive our frailty :
We have of late lacked sugar in our dish,—
Have had sour falsehoods served to us for sweetmeats;
So our sharp tongue grows as a ready spoon,
To serve to 'em others.

LADY.

        Will you go with me
To mirth's refection ?

HYLAS.

     We want appetite
For dished-up festals.   When we grow a-hungered,
We will come forth and lick the emptied salvers.
We are the dog, who were so late the darling.

LADY.

The lapdog, then.   You shall lie in my lap,
If you will follow yonder.

HYLAS.

     No, Delilah;
Not thus into the hands of the Philistines.—
Nay, grow not wroth, though I have grown profane;
Let me propitiate your dryad lips,—
Approach those dread divinities, your eyes,
That roll their pomp, enshrined on living thrones

Of casing alabaster. 'Tis your eyes
That have matured your lips, even as Apollo's
Mature the summer fruitage, and the glances
Of the sheet-lightning the autumnal corn.
Your eyes are fountains of empyreal fire,
Whereat we stand, and, warming us, admire.

LADY.

Your highness still admires your own eyes most.

HYLAS.

Never so much as in the glass of yours.

LADY.

Fie! if your highness will accompany me,
As stars admire themselves in hundred waves,
You shall admire your eyes in hundred ladies'.
Let us descend unto the terrace, where
The Duke is seated; he enquires for you.
See how the waving limes are beckoning;
The poplar too, the churchman's favorite tree;
And the half-everlasting cedars, grave
Do nod obeisance at your coming forth.

HYLAS.

The Duke, who sent you, surely knew your worth.
Tell him we've taken horse.   [*Exit abruptly.*

LADY.

                  Did ever colt
So break away while he was being curried?
Is this our late gallant and courteous prince?
What hath that vain and cunning countess done!
He is bewitched: not Acteon so started
When on himself Diana set his hounds.
He started from me as he'd heard the hounds,
With "hark-away," as sudden as a crack,
To leap the countess, proud Volina's, pale.
Oh, wicked greediness of that wed woman!
Not satisfied to rule the minister,

She must attract, with eye malign, from court,
The prince, to dark and secret chamberings.
Out on the wallowing, wanton sorceress!
Out on such change of nature in Lord Hylas!
The warm west wind that breathed so kindly on us,
Changed to the chapping north, or gloomy east.
Oh, slander, vilest slander! 'tis not we,
But men, that are inconstant. He who late
Was an acknowledged, though delightful, pest,
With toy and pastime, to most buxom ladies,
Indifferent before me now can stand,
Lolling like to a languid invalid,
And rolling lazy eyes with strange no-meaning;
Telling me, even to my very nose,
That I had ceased to charm him.—Lack-a-day!
What to the Duke his father shall I say?

SCENE VI.

A room in FILIPPO's *mansion. Time, following that of the last scene.*

VOLINA.

Oh, wretched to be thus compelled to look
Into the darkness that contains the ghost!
These straying thoughts will not be kept at home;
But, as the flies, though beaten thence, resort
Where careful housewife storeth up her sweets,
Forbidden, they do still revert to Hylas.
Oh, Hylas, Hylas, wherefore have I known thee?
Out of my thoughts; begone, or, with thine image,
So fill me that there be no room for conscience!
                                    [*Enter a* PAGE.

PAGE.

My lady, the Lord Hylas seeks admittance.

VOLINA (*aside*).

We will feign sickness, or will be abroad:—
And yet not that.—[*Aloud.*] Go bid him hither, boy.
                                    [*Exit* PAGE.

G

Hither he comes; and, oh, how wild, how wan!
How hath the love-god bled him with his arrows!
Freeze, thawing heart; grow sudden dry, moist eye.

[Enter HYLAS.

Unwelcome! [*aside*] yet as welcome as the dew.
Aloud.]   Your highness, wherefore will you test me thus?
Why force me still to use unkindest terms?

HYLAS.

And wherefore should you use them?   Albeit chide me,
I will not answer; hate me, if you will,
And I your hatred will requite with love.

VOLINA.

Do I, then, look as though I hated you?
Still, if you love me, as you say you do,
Even for that love's sake tarnish not my fame
By these forbidden but repeated visits.

[VOLINA going, the PRINCE falls on his knees to stay her.

HYLAS.

Love you, Volina?   Oh, how much, how madly,
Let the swollen mountain of my grief, and these
Swift, tear-worn gullies in my cheeks, declare.
Forbid me not to plead: beholding, hear me;
Hear me, Volina; hear and pity me.
See me before you, wan for lack of sleep;
Wasted and lean for lack of appetite;
Despising recreation, scorning dress;
Hating the light,—all hating save yourself;
And more than all—

VOLINA.

Begone, or else let me go!

HYLAS.

Thou beautiful Volina, peerless woman,
As honor is an attribute of man,—

VOLINA.

Oh, thou dishonorable piece of beauty!—
Nay, now I hate, far more than fear, you.   Honor?

Honor is none where honor is unwelcome;
A guest that never stays to be dismissed,—
Departing ere the lips may mould the breath
That gives him his congé.

HYLAS.

'Twere but a brief, but momentary lapse.

VOLINA.

'Twere to be damned for ever.   Must I frown?
Oh, could I frown thee from me!

HYLAS.

              'Tis in vain:
You shine the more, the more you call on clouds,
That will not come; but in their stead appear
Sheet lightnings that envelop you, until
You shew more glorious than a crownèd queen.
Ah, would you were my queen, my duchess, wife!—
Oh, be my mistress!—Wherefore do you start?
You shall not live and die in durance, then
Be cast out for the worm to banquet on;
But be as one from false imprisonment plucked
To liberty and life, for you are dead
And buried in a union lacking love.
You do not love your husband,—nay, you do not;
Hence the sweet deed you do with him so saintly,
What is it more than bitterness and sin?—
Nay, if you weep, you conquer me again,
Breaking my hard heart with those hailstone tears.

VOLINA.

Will you not leave me?

HYLAS.

           Not while you are thus,—
Why should you fear the snake that you have charmed?
Forgive me my most deep and dire offence.

VOLINA.

I have offended too;—but go for ever.

HYLAS.

Say you not hate me : be your last look kind.
Volina, lovely, much-insulted woman,
Shake me not off.   Believe, the ivy is
Not chaster when it clings unto the wall;
Nor the fair-fingered honeysuckle, when
She pinneth her festoons upon the oak ;
The south wind playing round virgin violets
Guiltier than now my fancy for your form.

VOLINA.

Will you begone ?

HYLAS.

For aye ?

VOLINA.

For aye.

HYLAS.

'Tis done.

The storm is passed, or lulled : yet, ere we say
Adieu, together, to compose ourselves,
Let us abroad to walk where yonder boughs
Twine melancholy dim ; or let us sit
Where, deep in yonder vista, the brown old,
Tranquility, outspreads her mossy seat.
There let us sit and sigh, or ere we sever ;
There let us sigh, for we must sigh for ever.

[*Exeunt.*

SCENE VII.

—

A room in GONARDO'S *house.   Time, following that of the last scene.*
GALLANTIO *and* PAPHIANA.

GALLANTIO.

Now let the drums roll muffled ; let the bells'
Shrill tongues toll mournfully for Hylas slain.
But though all nature should put mourning on,
Though drums be garnished with funereal crape,

My brows shall wear no less their native rose;
Though rusty drops should from the bells descend,
Dappling the upturned throats of thirsty ringers,
Adown mine own nb less red wine shall flow.
We'll pledge the genius of ill luck,—why not?
And draw bright laughter out of dull defeat.

PAPHIANA.

Thou hast a nobler spirit than the prince.—
But is it true he plays the moribond?

GALLANTIO.

Dead, dead! shot, shot to death, Paph, shot.
Yes, fairly shot, all foully shot, hath been
This representative of thirty dukes;
Each a contemner both of dart and gun.
Dead, dead is Hylas; shot, young Hylas, shot;
Banished into the air, Paph; blown point blank
Into the world-wide welkin, shattered, shivered.
All shattered, shivered, shot; oh, shooting shame!
Shot with the bombshell of Volina's eyelid.

PAPHIANA.

See here the power of woman when she wills.

GALLANTIO.

True, you are powerful, and can sting like nettles,
When you are plucked by over-fearful fingers.
Volina hath her would-be stinger stung;
Teased him, as a tormenting wasp or bee
Might, in the flowery meadow, tease the steer;
Bled him to death, as butcher might a calf,—
Full many a calf hath less deserved the butcher,
Full many a butcher better quitted Cupid;
Who's shot my blue-eyed booby out of ambush;
Couching, like painted Indian 'midst the reeds,
In covert of Volina's dark eyelashes.
Now let him puff with pride of sovereign blood.
Oh, sovereign blood! oh, blood of thirty sovereigns!

Who now would give a penny for a pint
Of sovereign blood ? Paph, not a pint of blood
Is in his carcass left, with love-shot riddled.

PAPHIANA.

The hunter's self hath e'en been hunted down,—
The deer he stalked hath given him a gore.

GALLANTIO.

Most grievously hath gored him ;—but I've lost
Now faith in elegants ; believe what's told
Of stalwart Samson by Delilah bound ;
Of Hercules to spinning set with maids ;
Of Jacob, too, who twice seven years to Laban
Did bind himself apprentice for his wives.
These bonds are good, since Hylas hath endorsed them.

PAPHIANA.

These all are holy writ. But something, perhaps,
Has been forgotten in the prince's mould ;
As in his ducking was Achilles' heel.

GALLANTIO.

He 's no Achilles, though she is a Helen,—
No Cæsar he, though she as Cleopatra ;
Volina lonely lingering in her bower,
Rose pillowed, match for Egypt's magic queen.—
But as Marc Antony did lose the world
To win grand Cleopatra, so hath Hylas
Now lost his heart but hath not won Volina.

PAPHIANA.

Beware of Filippo when he returns.

GALLANTIO.

We are as one who carries a dark-lantern,—
Unseen ourselves, yet seeing others.

> [*A bell tolls at a distance.*
> Hist !

It is the note for my departure.

PAPHIANA.

Thou

Dost know it well, as doth the trooper know
The call to boot and saddle. Get thee gone.
Remember me.   [*Exit.*

GALLANTIO.

A man may grow too famous;
Else had there been herein no need of helper.
My character hath grown unto mine aims,
As is its rattle to the rattlesnake.
As is its attribute, to that most fatal
Serpent, a warning to its prey, so is
My bad report a warning grown to woman.
Blessed is the man of reputation sound;
But my free life hath drilled mine as the moth,
Till I am even as one attired in rags,
With whom none will consort for very shame.
I would I had an angel's coat of light,
To wrap me wherewithal!
But forth, and lightly let my footsteps fall.   [*Exit.*

SCENE VIII.

—

The grounds of FILIPPO'S *mansion, contiguous to those of* GONARDO.
Time, following that of the last scene. Enter HYLAS *and* VOLINA.

HYLAS.

Oh, might now time stand still, or but one step
Pace farther, when, methinks, we should have come
Even to the very verge and brink of bliss!
Why dost thou tremble? All the air is still;
The vine sleeps, and the aspen quivers not;
The stars wink under the cloud's coverlid;
The moon, abed, sleeps on Endymion's breast;
Earth mingles in a dim embrace with heaven.
                        [*Exeunt, and enter* GONARDO.

GONARDO.

Better here than in my house,—better to greet
The heaven's true stars, than those false eyes at home.
The kiss o'the wind polluteth not my cheek;
These leaves, with their green lover-lips, pour not
Deceit into mine ear.   And yet forgive
Me, if herein I haply err.   Most men,
When doubtful of the virtue of their wives,
With some contrived restraints will hedge them in;
But I have oped the paddock gate to mine.
But may this course, if wrong, be pardoned, both
Of honor and of Heaven.   Still befriend me,
Thou darkly-staining juice, and, ye wild weeds,
Hide me as armour hides the vizored knight;
Still, ye Bohemian garments, cover me,—
Better by you be covered than by shame.

[Enter GALLANTIO.

GALLANTIO.

Whither have I stumbled?   'Tis a pitch-dark night;
Yet should I know Gonardo's grounds.

GONARDO.

I know the owner of that voice too well:
It is the very villain that we seek,—
The very form that fills our big suspicion.

GALLANTIO.

But these grounds are the Count's.   I dare not hollow;—
Yet soon will hollow in their owner's ear,
Through a quill trumpet, when, although the blast
Sound to a false alarm, the sleeping warden
Shall, waking, think the castle has been sacked.

GONARDO.
Will he betray the prince?

GALLANTIO.
            The hyps keep Hylas;
He is a poor, emasculated knave,—
No genuine crystal, but mere glittering ice,—

Who, when a glorious woman shines upon him,
As the sunned ice goes trickling to the gutter,
Dissolves away into clay-tempering tears.

GONARDO.
Would that were true!

GALLANTIO.
                    Poor goose! were now the Count,
Gonardo, and his countess, Paphiana,
I had out-counted him amidst the flock,
Then hissed him off the common.

GONARDO.
                    Must I hear it?
I'll draw and drink the blood o'the miscreant!—No,
Let him espouse her, let him gobble her up;
Ay, let him hang her, hang her, even hang her,
So mine estate be charged not with the noose.

GALLANTIO.
The Count will soon return.

GONARDO.
                    So will Gonardo.

GALLANTIO.
All will be over then.

GONARDO.
                    With thee, with thee.

GALLANTIO.
'Tis hard to have failed; but it must even be so.

GONARDO.
How resignation sits upon the wolf!
Worse than the cloak of little Red Ridinghood.

GALLANTIO.
The lion loves not to repeat its spring.

GONARDO.
The ass disdains not to repeat its kick.

GALLANTIO.

My carrion dudgeon must I now devour.

GONARDO.

Worse than the thorniest thistles will it be.
May 't stick amidst thy throat, thou boa-constrictor!
May'st choke thee with the dudgeon's poking horns!

GALLANTIO.

'Twill disagree with me,—'twill gripe, 'twill gripe.

GONARDO.

May 't poison thee!—rat, may it rid us of thee!

GALLANTIO.

Why, let it gripe, so he be wrung with colic.
He shall be caught with stitches in the side;
The old fool shall be cramped and doubled up,
'Till he shall gasp for breath, and gnash his teeth
Sheer through his lips in deep, dumb agony.
We'll write until the saint's old sinews crack,—
We'll write to him to put him on the rack.   [*Going*.

GONARDO.

Not so we part: 'tis my divining hour;
I'll run my brigantine across his forefoot,
Though loathing commerce with the red-eyed wretch,
That wends through night as Phlegethon flows through hell,
His blood impregnate with lascivious fire.
Nature hath labelled him a lecher, and
Debauchery foul blurred his person o'er,
Wiping at last her pen upon his face.
Faugh! can a woman love such unclean beast?
Darkness, dispose thy mask on both our charms.
We'll softly sing him to these syren arms.

[*Trolls*.

Heigh, for the hall of the greenwood,
And the wind-wagged faggot fire;
And the piping pot, with the game we have got
From the covers of the squire.
The piping pot, with the game we have got,
What more can man require?

II.

Sweet rove the moonlit greenwood,
Sweet dance about the tent;
Sweet lie beneath, with wife, on heath,
And pay nor rack nor rent.
To lie beneath, with wife, on heath,
Who would not be content?

GALLANTIO.

Ho, nightingale!

GONARDO.

What would your honor with me?

GALLANTIO.

Is this green copse your cage? Come, troll again.

GONARDO.

[*Song.*

The gallant to the gypsy said,
Tell me my fortune, pray:
I wish to slumber in the bed
Of a certain lady gay.

II.

The lady seems not hard to win,
Nor hard to win am I;
Then tell me if I ever in
The lady's bed shall lie.

GALLANTIO.

Good! Thou shouldst read my hand, were't not now night.

GONARDO.

The face, sir, is a worthier instrument;
The notary, Nature, having quaint engrossed
Thereon each mortal's legacy of life.

GALLANTIO.

'Tis night, 'tis night,—a night as dark as death.

GONARDO.

Say not 'tis night, your unknown worthiness:
'Tis day where shines your countenance, that, like

The sun's, is legible by its own beams.
Your face is luminous as passionful,
Signal as if it had been chalked with phospher.

GALLANTIO.

Thou knowest me.

GONARDO.

Who cannot tell a gentleman by night,—
The glowing, gallant blood athwart the dark ?
Your nobler crafts that navigate the land,
Still carry evening lights upon your bows ;
Upon your fronts you cavaliers bear beams
That cannot be extinguished by the gloom.

GALLANTIO.

What of our face ?—no further fooling with us.

GONARDO.

It is a link-boy to your lordship,—lighting,
Sometimes, your way into a lady's bower.

GALLANTIO.

How knowest thou we are noble ?

GONARDO.
            By your voice.

GALLANTIO.

We are not noble, but most reverend.

GONARDO.

Then pity you have taken orders ; for
Your reverence loves the ladies.   To the fair,
You had been Gog and Magog with that face :
All over it old capricorn crops out.

GALLANTIO.

We are nor Gog nor Magog, but the devil.
Darest read i'the dark the face of Lucifer ?

GONARDO.

Be not offended if I read as written.
Here great concupiscence, there little love :

The latter disappearing very soon
Beneath the former; as a dead, white babe,
Whose restless, drunken nurse has overlaid it.

GALLANTIO.

'Twould seem too dark to read this scroll of flesh.

GONARDO.

It is a fine illuminated missal,
And many a maiden must have said her prayers
Therefrom when you were younger; many a wife
Repeat now thence love's Latin litany.
It were as good as to have built a church,
To have fashioned such a visage. Blessed sire,
Thrice-blessed mother, to have built such church;
Oh, strangest church, wherein, like ugly demons,
Husbands may sourly sit, and 'gainst their wives
Dole the dark collect of hard commination!—
But what perceive we on it? You love a lady
Whose husband lieth at the door of death.

GALLANTIO.

Is that written on our face? We must begone:
Here's for thy songs, old mole.   [Gives GONARDO money.

GONARDO.

'Twere labor cast away to part so soon.
     [Exit GALLANTIO, and GONARDO throws the money from him.
Thus may thy soul be cast away at judgment!
Old mole? I yet will be his mole, his mauler;
Even yet will prove a mole amidst his meadow;
Will secret work; will undermine his path,
'Till, as the mole's, my track shall only show
Where lies the upthrown havoc.
                    [Enter HYLAS and VOLINA.
                Gleams of ghosts!

HYLAS.

A little farther, yet a little farther.
'Tis sweet to wander thus, not caring whither,

So we keep company.   This hour was made
For us, as we were surely for each other.

[*Exeunt, having crossed the stage.*

GONARDO.

Oh, grief on grief! oh, pair of faithless wives!
Now surely Paphiana must be gnawed,
When this transcendent robe betrays the moth.
Alas! alas!   Ah, twice alas 'tis now;
Twice being bound bear witness 'gainst my neighbour,—
Not falsely, nor in malice, Heaven knows,
But seeking evidence in mine own cause;
As he who, searching criminal archives,
Stumbles on proof of unsuspected crime.
Oh, hapless I, to stumble on such crime!
Oh, hapless men, Gonardo, Filippo!
Oh, wicked, wayward, hapless, wanton women;
Sad pair of perpetrators in one guilt;
Foul breakers both of blest connubial oaths.
But what are oaths to bind the lawless blood?
Who now shall eulogize the twofold cord?
All marriage-cords are spun of rotten hemp,—
Ne'er Hymen's chains were forged without a flaw!
Talk of connubial love, domestic treasures;—
Love's treasures in one bottom may be lost,
Sunk on the shallows of shame's shoreless sea,
Leaving but one poor floating plank of hate.
Oh, love, thou symbol of the various world,
As it hath black banditti and corsairs,
Thou hast thy libertines, adulterers.
Ah, me! ah, me! now heavier seems my lot,
Seeing such burden binding for another.
Now never more may we believe in woman!
Who would have deemed Volina, angel fair,
Could have been coupled in the same foul leash
With my corrupt, offending, spotted hound?
Oh, universal spot! oh, stain, hath struck,

As a strong blemish through a volume's leaves,
From Eve through all her daughters until now !
Now let be blessed held celibacy ;
The marriage state be held a state at war.
As merchant fleets do need an armed convoy,
The married man should be a man-at-arms.
Licentious man,—weak woman, fair while firm,—
Alas, beyond the art of words to paint
Thy threefold gorgon foulness in thy fall !
We'll write to Filippo more plainly now ;
We must his honorable bosom trouble :
Refraining, were her crime, his woe, to double.
Let me begone, sick with this saddening sight.
Come, horror's foot, and bear us through the night.   [*Exit.*

SCENE IX.

The Ducal Palace at Arno. FILIPPO *reading a letter.*

FILIPPO.

" I write to you now in no enigma : the matter is too plain.
I speak of what I saw. When the sun retires behind the cloud,
what eye shall follow, what fingers undraw his burning curtain ?
                                        " Yours,   ————,"

A second dart from an invisible hand !
Who sends to me these terrible despatches,
That make a stop-watch of my beating heart,
With visionary-fingered, sad impression,
That here at Arno's goal my race is run ?
Down, black presentiments ;
Hence, miserable, monster-mouthed conjectures !
I will not listen, will not cherish doubt,
Since doubting of my wife were to condemn her,
As willing, if not fallen, to offend.
Yet wives have sometimes so offended ;—true ;

And youth is prone to trespass against age,
Breaking the reins of reverence. No; my wife,
As fillies sometimes run off with the halter,
May have been guilty of some indiscretion
Of youthful spirits' prompting;—nothing more:
Yet here see "clouds" and "burning curtains." Ah,
This light, though dim, is yet too dazzling. Hath
Seraphio been remiss? or hath he touched
(As might a bounding vaulter's toe the stage)
Pereza's point too briefly, in his zeal
To bring relief to my disquietude?
I am perplexed, bent, paralyzed by doubt;
Slain, with no sign of wound upon my form,
By the mere wind of paper cannon-ball.
Oh, now Vesuvius rests upon a worm!
Now doubt disables me, up-piles my load,
Yet cuts the sinews of the back that bears it.
What must be done? up by my sense'one rose
Springs the sharp thorn.—I'll pluck thee up soon, thorn.
Home, home to my true wife! she must be true;
Must not be basely thus suspected. Yet—
Yet if, indeed, she hath let loose the tempest
That may unroof and lay me in dishonor,—
Hath set me in the zodiac of the age,
A lofty butt for laughter to the young,
Unto the old a sighing.—But we rave;
These lines were penned by some malicious hand.
Set, sun, at once, that sheds such long, grim shadows!

[*A* Page *enters with another letter; and, having delivered it to* Filippo,
retires.

[*Breaking the seal.*

Why do I tremble, as though this contained
A creature that might spring upon and sting me?

[*Reads.*

"You are dishonored: your wife, whom you believed to be
invincibly virtuous, yields herself up in assignations. A youth
(most beautiful—some say it is an angel in disguise—would that

they played none but celestial pranks !) visits her, boasting to my
secret ear their deeds.

"Your most unwilling informant, ————."

Crack on crack ! let all thy flames loose, sky ;
Burn until bloodshot grows the blue-eyed welkin.
Now is it wrong to stay for Plumio's death,
When, be these doubled admonitions true,
Is worse than death,—ay, or damnation too.

SERAPHIO (*entering*).
Plumio is dead !

FILIPPO.
Is he released at last ?
Convey his corse back with you to Pereza.
I thither start forthwith : ask me not why.

SERAPHIO.
In coming hither from poor Plumio's room,
I met a seignior, instant from Pereza,
Who says your lady from her frighted steed
Was lately rescued by a cavalier,
Else were she dashed to pieces.

FILIPPO (*aside*).
Dash away,
I've got amongst the breakers.

SERAPHIO.
So, 'twould seem,
Your dream, so ominous, had root in nature.

FILIPPO (*aside*).
Grant not such deep root as henceforth to fill
With weed of woe my life's henceforward field !
Aloud.] There is much more in dreams than yet is dreamed of.
What further did he tell you of my wife ?
Pray you reserve not from me aught of evil.

SERAPHIO.
You have not lost, then, your presentiment.

H

FILIPPO.

Not quite, not quite. Who was this rescuer?

SERAPHIO.

I know not; but your lady will inform you,
Doubtless, with grateful joy.

FILIPPO.

Even so.
Aside.] All cannot feign,—three witnesses,—for I
Will not accept mere dream as evidence;—
Yet may these three be one; perchance some villain
Attempting, both with mouth and pen, to abuse me.

SERAPHIO.

I leave you to prepare.

FILIPPO.

We thank you.   But
Who told you of Volina's late escape?

SERAPHIO.

His name I know not. He was passing through,
And now is far beyond this.

FILIPPO.

'Tis no matter.
                         [*Exit* SERAPHIO.
She loves me,—I am certain that she loves me!
True, she indeed will sometimes chafe, secluded,—
Will sue to me for gayer company;
True, she is sometimes cold, and even sullen,—
Oft stints me at the table of her body,
Whereat, so fair, an angel might exceed.
Still, what of that?   I am not young as she,—
Yet from the first she knew it.   True indeed,
Heaven hath denied us children; but instead
Hath given us grace to patiently endure
To lack love's crown and blessing.

SERAPHIO (*re-entering*).

                         Pardon me;
For your content I have enquired the name

Of my informant: one Pallazzo 't is.
His servant journeyed with him, and told mine
Gonardo's lady visits at your house;
So that your wife hath not lacked company.

FILIPPO (*aside*).

This salve 's a biting blister. [*Aloud.*] Aught beside?

SERAPHIO.

'Twas rumoured in Pereza, when he left it,
Gornardo had expired, I think in Rome;
Poor man! you know that he was jealous; still,
So far as I believe, he had no cause,
Save that his wife was buxom, and the bloated
Gallantio (and who that's fair and woman
Doth he not gaze on?) oft would gaze upon her.

FILIPPO.

Insatiate wretch!—Go on; what further news?

SERAPHIO.

None further;—e'en the veriest trifles these,
Scarcely worth while their bringing.

FILIPPO.

Thanks for them;
And greater thanks for the most kind intent,
That gives a cultivation and a fragrance,
Beyond their native comeliness and worth,
To these stray wild-flowers you have gathered for me.
[*Exit* SERAPHIO.
They smell not sweet though: here Gonardo dead,
His wife (or rather widow now) become
Familiar with Volina. Never loved
We that same woman. To my soul,
Ill omens, perching, come upon her name,
And cry and clamour till my heart's red hall
Quakes to its fixed foundation. Says the saw,
"Birds of a feather"—what 's the saw to me?
Lock me, ye eyelids, up these visual balls;

Nor further read the proverb, trite as true.—
What is to me the adage, or to her?
Volina is unsullied as the swan
That plumes its white breast in the limpid flood,
Or cygnet without speck; chaste is she as
The lonely phœnix that engenders not,
Renewed from forth its own unsexual fires;
Splendid as gorgeous bird of paradise,
Yet true as homeliest songster to its mate.
She shall not be suspected, beautiful;
We will not, as we purposed, straight to horse,
But stay to slowly follow Plumio's corse.
                    [*Enter* VERTALDI, *a just-arrived Perezan noble.*
Ah, my dear Lord, what news now from Pereza?
We are upon the eve of our return;—
Not as we came, with empty car, wherein
To bear the uncertain answer to our suit,
But with that vacant car now overfilled,
Even with the added freightage of the dead:
My secretary hath this hour expired.

VERTALDI.

Alas! you loved him,—but who loved him not?

FILIPPO.

I did, all did; perhaps too much, too much,—
Almost as much as we should love our wives.
I would I were at home: all now seems flat;
My heart is chilly, and the hearth's bright warmth
Were its best comfort.—Ah, my lord, no spot
Like one's own house.—Why are you dumb?
Love you not home?

VERTALDI.

                    Report saith yours is haunted.

FILIPPO.

Then so but lately, if you mean by more,
Or worse, than the good angels, who I hope,
Do now, and will continually, guard it.

VERTALDI.

Amen.

FILIPPO.

You say "amen" as though there were much need on't.
What means your most mysterious emphasis?

VERTALDI.

Nay, nothing:—all of us do need protection;
And if my lips had proffered now your prayer,
I should not mind how deep were your amen.

FILIPPO (*aside*).

More is there here than lies upon the lips;
Something doth lurk at bottom of his eyes.
I'll dive for it, though bringing 't up should drown me.
Aloud.] What haunts my mansion say they? flesh and blood?

VERTALDI.

Ay, truly, nothing worse.

FILIPPO.

        Yet bad enough,
My lord, it might be; for within the range
And fixed frontiers of our humanity,
As on a scale, are found all grades between
God, open-eyed, and the sly, winking fiend.—
But tell me truly, is there aught amiss?
What meant you when you said my house was haunted?

VERTALDI.

Merely that you should know of such report.
How much it means I know not, nor what value
The bill my tongue hath drawn upon your credit.
So goes report.

FILIPPO.

        Report is but a dolt,
That takes for oracle the whispering wind,
Believes the blast to be the din of demons.
Describe to me this sprite; although it shew
Fouler than nightmare, or the Norway hag.

VERTALDI.

Its quality seems mystic.   Touching it,
There goes a running rumour in Pereza,
On hearing which they hush and look alarmed;
As when at nightfall's dumb and dusky hour,
Lone seated in some antiquated room,
Rise noises, coming from one knows not where;
Or, after some enquiring colloquy,
Stand serious gazing in each other's face,
Wherein they seem afraid to put their meaning.
These elements configure as you choose,
Or give them even no consideration;
But I have faster posted hither, bearing
This bag of breath, perhaps to you important,—
Or, yet as likely, all of import empty.
We now must take our leave: farewell.

FILIPPO.

Farewell, farewell; so, seignior, farewell.

                                        [*Exit* VERTALDI.

Come, fear, I will not drive thee from me now;
Strong-armed suspicion, come, and by the hair
Suspend me over the abyss of hell!—
But are there no more messengers a-coming?
Beat on, blow, wind from wilderness; blow, blow.—
Yet, Job, I cannot acquiesce as thou,—
Cannot think my love, my life, is ta'en away.
Yet must I bear this, must perforce endure.
These letters' faces now are wiped of much
Discredit by this napkin of report.
Oh, God! oh, Christ! oh, all-dispensing Heaven,
Why hast thou sent me this sharp portion down?
Where are ye, affidavits?   [*Taking out the letters.*
" A beauteous youth "!—Out eyes, or read no more!
" Some say it is an angel in disguise."
" Yields herself up in assignations ";—it is false!
She would not yield her to Apollo's arms,
Though she might well attract him from the skies.

Ah, would we were at home ! doubt, like the lever,
More powerful grows the farther from its fulcrum,
And somewhat do I doubt my love, even yet.
Their times so with these tidings coincide,
They form a riddle that must be resolved :—
Even now the Sphinx devours me.   Doubt it not,
Something hath loudly fallen in Pereza
When the reverberations reach to here.
As many streams, converging, form but one,
That falls into some boundless, foreign gulf,
Here lies a web of circumstance, whereof
Chance cannot be the weaver ; yet that I
Must aid to unravel, though dark Atropus
Therein should cut me with her shifting shears.
Mistrust is ill enough 'twixt man and man ;
But, 'tween the woman of our heart and us,
Lost confidence is even loss of all.
All may be lost : dream unto dream, and fact
To fancy corresponding, bar me rest.
I can no longer here abide in doubt,
No longer can I linger from my love.
Love cries "away !" crime creeps not toward its deeds ;
Back to Pereza on relays of steeds.

END OF THE FOURTH ACT.

ACT V.

SCENE I.

A room in FILIPPO'S *mansion.* VOLINA *sits weeping, with her face hidden in her hands.* HYLAS *stands near, regarding her.*

HYLAS.

Enough of tears, enough of tears, Volina.
Bid cease these showers, whose gushes hinder speech.
Cease, cease these sobs, that, ceasing not, will end us
With double dissolution; since with thee
I die, I live. Fear not, my life, my love;
My joy, my jewel: Hylas will protect thee.
Calm thee, my dearest; look upon me; speak.
Speak, speak, Volina; speak to thine adorer.
Oh, seal those penitential fountains up:
'Tis sin to oversorrow even for sin.
Let there at length be drought.   Let me now wipe
The ooze from round those sorrow-stricken eyes;
Dry with my breath, as with warm wind of June,
The cold, drenched pavement of those marble cheeks.

VOLINA.

Oh, come not near me, Hylas: I am foul!
I cannot look upon thee for sheer shame;
I would not speak but that thou dost compel me.
I cannot look the daylight in the face;
How shall I meet my husband's angry eyes?
Snatch me from Filippo or ere he come;
Hide me where night perpetually reigns.
Death, death, come thou and overshadow me;
Sail o'er this desert heart, thou vulture, death,
And pick this erring beauty to the bones.

HYLAS.

Oh, horrible expressions !

VOLINA.

What are the words that can express me fully ?
What language, all voluminous and large,
Could hold my bulk of guilt and misery ?
Let, let me rave,—or, rather, e'en be dumb,
For perfect silence doth express me best.

HYLAS.

Then must I sit down by you, as Job's friends
Did sit by him until he oped his mouth.
Be it seven days, or be it seven years,
Or let it stretch out to eternity,
I will not leave you maddening.

VOLINA.

   Must I speak ?

HYLAS.

Say what you wish me do :—and, though it were
Impossible ; make null old Nature's law ;
Revoke, or change, or turn aside our own,—
Which I may do for your sake when I'm duke,—
All, all, save to renounce you, is performed.

VOLINA.

Then shield me from my husband ; pity me,
Whom thou hast ruined, help whom thou hast hurt.
Let me not sue in vain ; a little while
Assist me. See me changed ; humble, indeed ;
Abject thou seest me, I so lately proud ;
Fallen, low fallen, I so lately high ;
Poor, I so lately rich in admiration :
Then do not thou desert me, wrecked by thee ;
Oh, stay by me and save me, once deemed costly ;
Now, if thou scorn me, valueless indeed !

HYLAS.

We both are stranded,—both upon cold beach
Awhile must stand, like shivering castaways ;

But, with the broad sail of Pereza's power,
I soon shall shelter thine exposèd head.
And, oh, my treasure, over whom I joy,
As one who with his life hath saved his fortune
Out of the jaws o'the wave, to this fond heart,
Howe'er the world esteem thee, thou art dear
As Indies are to Spain; to these fond eyes,
Though in thine own defiled, appearest still pure.
Be comforted, we both have much offended,
Both been much tempted, which may be as breeze
To blow away some grossness from our guilt,
And, cutting, bring the tears into the eyes
Of a censorious world.

VOLINA.

Fond casuist,
Will the world judge as thou dost? will it weigh
The fors and the againsts in nicest scale,—
The soul's resistance 'gainst temptation's force?
And yet, perchance, some will; but the mad main,
Including the full jury of my sex,
Condemning me,—for thou shalt much escape,—
Will execrate. One also will be less
Their pity than their jest, my husband:—oh,
There is the thorn that runs into my heart!

HYLAS.

There lies the rack whereon myself am stretched.—
But let us steer from this afflictive shoal
Or ere we are aground on grief again.
How shall I serve you?

VOLINA.

Bear me swiftly hence;—
But, oh, whereunto? whither? My stern sire
Would shut the door against his erring child,—
He who himself provoked that child to err,
By bargained nuptials with Filippo;
While mother, sister, brother, have I none;
And, had I, they—oh, they, too, would disown me.
Lost! lost! Alas, where shall I shelter find!

HYLAS.

To-night you leave this place, and in the palace,
In secresy, which there is well obtained,
Immediately abide.

VOLINA.

The palace ? no,
Not to the palace, not unto the palace,—
And yet how oft have I not pined to go there !—
Not to the palace, Hylas ; no, not thither.
The palace ? no, no ; find me a lone cot,
Concealed by woods and girt by deep morass,
Where, undiscovered, I may live forgot.—
No, not unto the palace !

HYLAS.

'Twere most secret ;
For who would think of searching for you there ?

VOLINA.

Take me not thither.

HYLAS.

Fear no busy pryer,—
No marshal sent in quest to find you out.
There, privately, and in all honor, dwelling,
What time the present moments ripple by,
We will with the invention of true hearts,
Dig some deep channel for our future years.

VOLINA.

Dig me some deep, damp cell.—The palace ! oh,
Is that your sole asylum ? Does this dukedom
Contain no nook, no hole, no cave, no den ?
Is there no refuge in all Italy ?
Is there no covert in this big, vast world ?

HYLAS.

None like the one we proffer.

VOLINA.

Take me thither,—
Bear me where'er you will, since I must fly.

Lead me where'er you choose; I follow, so
You lead me to some place of fair repute.
Oh, to have this to bear !
But more must yet be borne ere all be done.

HYLAS.

Volina, through this day so bear yourself,
As though you were yourself of yesterday,
Till I to night returned convey you hence.
Farewell,—the saddest note in all love's gamut.
One relic kiss to charm this sorcerer sadness.
Nay, do not shrink from me; as might the tree,
If it had feeling, from the pruner's knife.

VOLINA.

Hylas, thou pluck'st from these lorn lips no more.
The stricken tree itself must quickly fall,
So fast at root 'tis rotting.   Rain nor sun
May e'er restore it, that again it bear
Fruitage of pleasure; but instead, its boughs
Black laden bending with harsh crabs of pain.

HYLAS.

'Twas wrong: caresses now are out of season.—
Still, fan away these croaking, raven thoughts,
Darker than night, or sable monkish guise
In which to-night we may salute your eyes.
'Till night adieu.

VOLINA.

                'Till night adieu.   [*Exit* HYLAS.
                    [*Rising.*] Till, till night?
There is no till where it is ever now ;
Now, now is night in this bedarkened soul.
Come, Nature's night, less dark than is my soul;
Eldest of things arrive and bear me hence,
Self-stricken from the morning welkin, down
To thine eternal arms !   Ah, me ! so young,
So early to be quenched ; so to have been
Upon the Orient, 'midst Aurorean light,
Caught by the Dis of Darkness !   Darkness, come,

Or ere comes Filippo; dread Filippo
As Darkness, dread as Dis; himself a Dis
When he to our domestic Enna came,
And gathered me its sole and young-eyed flower.
Ah, luckless bloom, unfortunatest flower!
Ah, dark the day I charmed his soul with form,—
When mere complexion turned the wise to folly!
What art thou, beauty, wonder-worker, what?
A fatal feof, a showy snare, at best,—
A morning sunbeam, in whose yellow breath
Creatures come bask and pipe, but, being gone,
Arcadia changes to a desert heath;
Light let into a room, whereon the flies
Enter and make their gratulative hum,
But, being withdrawn, as quickly they desert.
So when disease draws beauty's curtains down,
Slow-pacing years life's evening shutters close,
Sworn lovers and admirers due withdraw,
Going when goes that which they loved, admired.
Not such could Filippo have proved;—but why,
Ah, why hath Filippo admired and loved me?
Ah, wherefore have I married Filippo?
My father bade me, and my mother, she
Who should have sheltered,—shame, vile shame!—even she
Basely beseeched me; while, unto myself,
(Nor was my girlish hope therein deceived,)
Filippo seemed so generous a fowler,
That I, like bird that feels it must be caught,
Cowered 'neath my suitor's lowered, approaching hand.
This was your doing, most mistaken parents!—
This thine achievement, most ambitious sire!
But learn, too late, that though my marriage bond
By thee was signed in church, it still remains
Unsanctioned by my sacred Sire in heaven;
Hence hath it failed to hold these instincts, stronger
Than violent vows. But I grow violent;
Peace, peace, unfilial tongue;—yet why cry "peace,"
Where peace can never come? cry "war," cry "war,"

Yes wag tongue like a red-hot aspen leaf,
Against my sire, who once did tie thee up,
As one should wickedly tie up the tongue
Of the alarm-bell when the town's on fire;
Cry 'gainst a father that did quell my voice
When piteously it pleaded; did deny me
A maiden's native negative, and thrust
Me into Moloch's cage, wherein I shriek.
Now let me shriek, now let me howl o'er Hinnom,
'Till Calvery herself resounds with woe.
Oh, woe too great for woman! woe is me,
Bemoaning an inexpiable crime!
Whither shall I wander, wandering, bewail
This lapse?—oh, how escape worse plight than was
Eneas' midst the burning wreck of Troy?
Where? how?   Where'er I go is wrath, is I,—
This bursting breast as hollow Etna's side,
Beneath which rumbling fire and howling winds
Shake his brown, adamantine ribs, that hold
Chaos in chains, since mightier marriage chains
Have held not me!   Snap, chains, since I have snapped
Marriage's holy chain.   Burst, burning links of life;
Nature, dissolve, as hath dissolved my vow
As wax at fire of Hylas' youthful eye.
Ah, in that thought of youth what magic lies!
Had Filippo been young, or I, too, old;
Had both been young, or even both been old,
Had I but known the bliss of wooing,—that
Elysium I have missed, not lost; had I
Tasted of the sharp wine of winning eyes,
Eaten of the sweetness of the honeymoon,
Methinks I had been faithful: but instead,
Commanded, yea, expected to receive
A lord, (a lord how loving!) how could they
Expect a long allegiance?   Thirty years,
Unnatural difference in wedded pair!—
But man forgets his youth escapes with years,
As vapour from the pool 'neath summer suns.

Man that desires us for the sportive bed
Young, like the lamb provided for his board,
Forgets to marry while himself is young.
The male beast pairs in youth.   The male bird, too,
Is not a day the senior of his mate;
Man of life's sweetest season cheating his.
But all life's season now is o'er to me,
'Neath foot of trespass withered; all the field
Disdains me with its emerald eyes; the world's
Bright torch is out; around me all lies dark,
One only gleam plays feebly on heaven's verge,—
The hope of pardon.   Pardon will I seek;
Oh, heart, or ere 'tis granted do not break.   [*Exit.*

SCENE II.

*The Principal Street of Pereza. A Cathedral in the foreground, its bell
tolling. Enter* FILIPPO *in disguise, along with a citizen.*

CITIZEN.

You are a stranger in Pereza, then?

FILIPPO.

Look I not like one?—'Tis a noble street;
And handsome men and lovely women pace it.

CITIZEN.

Nor street nor pacers have elsewhere their equal.
See there the lady of Count Filippo,
Pereza's sun, the star of Italy.

FILIPPO (*aside*).

It is, it is my own mistrusted wife!

CITIZEN.

Not often she appears in public.   Never
Before have I beheld her thus afoot.
When she doth ride, her chariot seems a throne;
Nor hath the Duke two diamonds in his crown

To match her eyes, a fortune to her lord,
In contrast his rich fortune seeming poor.
You mark her closely: never saw you such.

FILIPPO (*aside*).

Suspicion, lull thee like a babe in arms.

CITIZEN.

As gilded mirror seems to don new pride
Before it passing some distinguished form,
So with her presence grows the street divine.

FILIPPO (*aside*).

She is not guilty; no, she is not foul!

CITIZEN.

She seems a-weary, sad: perchance she pines
For her now-absent lord.

FILIPPO (*aside*).

                    Within a month,
Could such a spirit turn to mire and clay?

CITIZEN.

I leave you, sir: you are pre-occupied.

FILIPPO.

We ill requite your courtesy; farewell.   [*Exit* CITIZEN.
All yet seems ominous; dread, drear, and dark.—
Lose not your hold, ye eyes. Whence comes this change?
Lo, heavily she treads, her settled gaze
Upon the ground, nor once upturned toward heaven.
Those limbs, so sprightly when I left them, now
Move slow as if bestruck with sudden age.
Is it sore sickness that hath sapped their strength?
Doth dull disease lie heavy on yon limbs,
Or do they bear the burden of a soul
Weighted with guilt too great to be forgiven?
Oh, for one word with her!—I will.—But what,
What questions would become this strange disguise?
My face would blab me too:—how hers is changed!—

In one mere moon changed even as the moon.
Another such sad change, 'twere death-like.—Oh,
My wife is sick, and I, I cruel here
Do stand and play the spy !

> [VOLINA *appears, and enters the cathedral.*
> She goes to shrift.—

Now omnipresent, yet forbearing, Heaven,
Forgive me if I do an impious act ;
But from her own, unconscious lips we now
Resolve us of her innocence or guilt.
What joy to listen to her silver tongue,
Outchiming nothing of illicit love !
I'll shrive her ; 'twere a sin to be forgiven.
Now follow straight, and be the ear of Heaven.

[FILIPPO *enters the cathedral, and* HYLAS *and* GALLANTIO *appear walking together : the cathedral bell still tolling.*]

GALLANTIO.

Your highness, shall your voyaging to and fro
But come to this, to beat the shallow shore,
And wreck your resolution 'gainst her charms ?
Would you, even yet, your wishes consummate,
You must bestir and strike, as strikes that bell,
Or Filippo's return will be your knell.

HYLAS.

What now the Countess Filippo to thee ;
Or unto me, in motion of dishonor ?
Begone ! Henceforwards we disown thee. If
Thou should'st obtrude thyself on us again
In street or palace, or i'the least defame
The lady of the absent Filippo,
Thou shalt have loosed on thee the muzzled law,
And long-pent thunder of our angry sire,—
Yea, go down foundering 'fore the wondering world.

> [*Enter* PAPHIANA.

PAPHIANA.

Good morrow, prince and peer.—What, do you quarrel ?

I

GALLANTIO.

Not we indeed : the prince hath pricked his finger.

[*Exit* HYLAS.

PAPHIANA.

What have you done, to anger thus the prince?

GALLANTIO.

Chidden the sinner for his wicked courses.—
Come, let us enter where the saints resort.

[GALLANTIO *and* PAPHIANA *enter the cathedral, and the scene changes to its
interior.* VOLINA *kneeling in silence before the confessional.* GALLANTIO
and PAPHIANA *at some distance.*]

FILIPPO (*within the confessional*).

Daughter, time presses, for the holy term
Draws near, when, with our common Christendom,
Pereza seeks to cleanse her from her sin.
What have you to divulge? what mortal stain
Contracted, that the precious blood of Christ
May wash not from your soul? What graces seek you,
That intercession of the Virgin Mother,
With prayers of saints auxiliar to your own,
May not obtain for you abundantly?
Speak, daughter: God is love; none need despair.—
You keep the primal virtue, chastity?

VOLINA.

I ought; but, oh, who do that which they ought?

FILIPPO.

Few; yet remember, if you have offended,
There was forgiveness even for Magdalen.

VOLINA.

May Heaven forgive me, too, for I do need it:
More heinous sin than Magdalen's is mine;
Adultery, worse than a virgin's lapse,—
Adultery, for that I need forgiveness.

FILIPPO.

So doth your paramour.

VOLINA.

Be it granted him !

FILIPPO.

He for himself must ask : no proxy here,
Which is as one with the great bar of God.
Deliver, first, into mine ear the name
(In custody for our most holy Church)
Of him who, knowing foul your married body,
Hath wronged its owner, even your husband, lord.

VOLINA.

His name ?—Oh, father, ask it not.   His name ?

FILIPPO.

Without it you can have no absolution.
It may go easier with him, should we know him;
Saving him penance, and yourself some pain.

VOLINA.

Whate'er it save me, I will not proclaim him !—
No absolution ?

FILIPPO.

       None, till you divulge
Who did assist you in this black misdeed.

VOLINA.

I have divulged, I have divulged the deed.
What matters a mere name ?—you cannot pain it,
You cannot set it penance, make it fast,
Nor send it far on perilous pilgrimage.

FILIPPO.

'Tis portion of your penance to pronounce it ;
Such crucifixion of Barrabas pride
Being the touchstone to your own remorse,
And my best leave to grant you absolution.
Think this not strange, nor needlessly severe,
Since, in these terrible enormities,
Heaven's upraised hand must not be lightly caught,
Lest we should draw upon ourselves the blow.
Declare by whom you fell, or I not shrive you.

VOLINA.

This were to lower fall!—You will not shrive me?
Oh, holy father, wherefore this strange rigor?
Lay all the fine and penalty on me:
I cannot, dare not, will not satisfy you.

FILIPPO.

Go, and think better of it.

VOLINA.

Nay.

FILIPPO.

You must.

VOLINA.

Cannot you shrive me else? I cannot tell thee;
Nor will I hence till I have absolution.

FILIPPO.

Away!

VOLINA.

Oh, horrible!—that voice!

[VOLINA *retires hastily from the cathedral, and* FILIPPO *comes forth.*

FILIPPO.

Break not, my heart, as yet; awhile forbear!
Oh, God! oh, God! Eyes, gush forth tears of blood.
Gaze not upon me, carven angel's eyes;
Or, if you will, turn me to stone like you.
Screen me, ye gloomy aisles; hide me, ye vaults.
Flow, tears; gush, flow; drown me. Oh, let me die!

PAPHIANA.

What frantic man is that?

FILIPPO.

She was a fiend, she was a fiend!—and yet
So beautiful, so bright, intelligent;
And if she had a dash of levity,
It did become her, as their wings do angels.

GALLANTIO.

What means the mouthing fool?

FILIPPO.

She never loved me :—now I understand
Her careless coldness,—yet, she could be hot,
Even with me.—Out, fabled chastity,
Thou woman's boast; out, live with wauling cats,
Monkeys, and goats.—Let me not yet go mad.

PAPHIANA.

See how he rolls his eyes ;—he laughs.

FILIPPO.

Ha, ha,
Now over her scared conscience I have hung
The very axe and bolt of sharp damnation.
She would not name her paramour ; but let her
Get shrift for money from some sharky priest.
I'll learn my wronger's name ; I'll force her yet
To write it for me with her rank, right hand.

GALLANTIO.

It is some lunatic.

PAPHIANA.

Poor creature, yes.

FILIPPO.

Faugh ! faugh ! the air yet stinks with her ; faugh ! faugh !
To have it, from the very culprit's lips,
Spawned in my ear.—Pah ! bring me holy water,
To wash out on't that word, adultery.
Oh, patience ! could I listen while she owned
That she herself, the palace of my pride,
Was entered, sacked.—Oh, damn her, damn her.

PAPHIANA.

Mark him.

GALLANTIO.

He's weeping now.

PAPHIANA.

What is his grief ?

Let us accost him.

GALLANTIO.

No, he has observed us:
See how he hies away.   [*Exit* FILIPPO.

PAPHIANA.

Poor fool, poor fool.

GALLANTIO.

Come, bird. [*Aside.*] Good for mine eyes this! Now I know
Yon seeming stranger was Count Filippo.

[*Exeunt.*

SCENE III.

Within the Ducal Palace at Pereza. DUKE, FIDEO, GONARDO [*not now in*
gypsy guise], COURTIERS, *and* OFFICERS.

DUKE.

Nay, 'tis a tale too wild to be believed,
As wild as is the weather,—Filippo
Returned from Arno, and in madman's mien!
Yet well he may, if what you say be true;
Which Heaven grant be not so, for the sake,
Not only of himself, but his sweet lady.
Oh, no, it cannot be she is corrupt!
So fresh, so taintless, the proud blue-fly roaming
Pereza's shambles still avoids her home,
As still the moth avoids the chest of cedar.
She is full safe, that most seraphic lady.—
True, angels fell without temptation, yet
She sits above the reach of its sharp dart.
What fly would fly so high as fly at her;
Who, as the lone and utmost flower on cliff,
That towers past flight of the thigh-laden bee,
Saves all its honey for the solar lips,
Now hoards herself for her returning lord?
Sirrah, if this be false you answer for it;—
Still, if you find Count Filippo, arrest him,
As well for safety, as that we may do

Our faithful minister justice, if he need it.
With him attach whoe'er you will, yourself
Warned 'gainst false seizures:—act you on these terms ?

GONARDO.

Most willingly, your highness.

DUKE (*to a courtier*).

Then, my lord,
Be at the bidding of this gentleman,
With such a force as he may choose, to-night.—
This passes our believing.—Hie away.
We wait on your returning as we may.

[*Exeunt* GONARDO *and courtier.*

Regard not all the story of this man,
Whose words have spotted this immaculate lady,
Even as God hath spotted the bright sun :
But count her stainless as the evening star ;
As far from folly as from fire is frost,
Or faintest bite of frost upon the sun.
She doth outvie the vain-eyed sun in beauty ;
So sweet a lady lives not in our realm.
Mind you not when she to our levee came,
The bride of Filippo ? Have you forgot,
How planet-struck gazed the gallants o'the court ;
How, wondering, its constellations waned ?
Why stand you all thus silent ?

FIDEO.

We are lost,
Your highness, in conjecture.

DUKE.

Dare you doubt her ?
Where are your knightly souls ? Oh, out !—and yet,
Alas, our own thoughts fill with gathering gloom ;
This heart sinks heavy.—Lead me to my room ;
There will we wait in prayer the dim event,
Eclipsing hope to pale presentiment.

Assist me now.—I quail with awe, not fright,
As something fatal would occur to night.—
Bear gently in your hands the living light:
Nigh ninety years 't has burned, and now we doubt,
Lest at some door the gust should puff us out.

        [*Exeunt, leading the* DUKE.

SCENE IV.

The grounds of FILIPPO's *mansion. Time, night. A violent storm of rain, thunder, and lightning. Enter* FILIPPO.

FILIPPO.

Though she be penitent and Heaven forgive her,
I cannot.   Out of my breast, relentings, out;
The heavens relent not, but pour bitterly.
Pour on, ye pitiless heavens, thou scowling sky;
Blow, bitter wind, less bitter than my grief;
Tear thy throat, tempest; thunder, peal
And terrify the welkin; lightnings, strike,
With your bright momentary blaze, sky's anvil,
Putting to blinder darkness time between.
Oh, heavy time, oh, darkened soul, oh, spirit,
Tossed wildly as yon woods.   Groan for me, woods,
Roar like the cataract, bow your proud heads,
As I am bowed; earth, rock till all grow dizzy.—
It is too foul, oh, 'tis too foul for pardon!

        [*Exit, and enter servants confusedly.*

FIRST SERVANT.

Come on, come on, boys; straggle altogether,
Each drabbled dog his tail between his legs.
Hasten; don't run about to every bush.
Here's wet enough, methinks, without your waters.

SECOND SERVANT.

Let the blind haste, and tumble in the ditch:
I'm blinded by this lightning.

FIRST SERVANT.

       Follow it,
And thou'lt grow nimbler.

THIRD SERVANT.

        Let him follow his nose,
That sallied 'fore us as a flaming rocket;
But now, rain-quenched, his best fun were to find it.
Sir, seek your nose.

FIRST SERVANT.

Come on, come on, cries Christy.   [*A peal of thunder.*

SECOND SERVANT.

Now were it good as ducats to be deaf.
I always had too sharp an ear for thunder.
Say, what is all this shooting up above?

THIRD SERVANT.

They're building in the sky, so shooting th' stones.

SECOND SERVANT.

Ha, ha, you stoney-head, you should be pelted
With your own jokes.

FOURTH SERVANT.

     Still fiercer flashes! These
Blue beams appear the opening eyes of hell.
Stay: here's some shelter.

   [*They all gather under a projecting ledge of rock.*
This storm abates not;—and, as I do live,
Antonio told me that this afternoon
He, in the environs, observed our master,
All in the torrent from the sheeted skies,
Wild, wet, and wan, upmuffled in a cloak,
Wandering about, like to a ghost forlorn.

FIRST SERVANT.

Andrea, likewise, even now told me
He saw one like him in the neighbourhood,
Who cast from time to time upon our house

Glances as terrible as were the lightnings;
Whose flashes did illuminate his face,
But which he neither seemed to fear nor shun.

SECOND SERVANT.

A lie, a lie, like that they told of me,
When they declared that they had caught me kissing
The blind old broom-woman 'neath my gabardine;
And heard the creature coaxing me to marry her,
Vowing to keep me like a gentleman
While she had breath or there were sale for brooms.
Truly but brooms were scarce, or I'd have swept
Their throats for 't.—You may laugh, but do you think
I dare prevaricate in this windy weather?
I fear God, too, as much as any man.
Who would offend Him in a tempest's teeth?—
All lies, all lies they've told you.

FIFTH SERVANT.

                        But for these
Same goblin stories, there are other vouchers:
Some of Gonardo's say that they beheld him,—
Ay, and Gonardo also not far off,
But in uncouth apparel, and as tanned
As he had been a voyage to the Indies.
                              [*Enter* GONARDO.

THIRD SERVANT.

Deuce knoweth where Gonardo is; but surely
Both his lone lady and our own, methinks,
Do lack alike their husbands.—I surmise
The Prince affects our mistress.

SECOND SERVANT.

                        Who shall say
That she stands unaffected?

FIRST SERVANT.

                        Blush you not
To whisper such a scandal, e'en by night?
You know not yet your mistress: check your tongues.

She holds the prince himself in awe,—could make
Him tremble at the shaking of her finger;
But for Gonardo's dame, and that vile rake,
Gallantio, if I surmise aright,
Each to the other holds the devil's candle.

GONARDO.

Lucifer light you, gentles!

THIRD SERVANT.

Saint Mark, bless us!

FIRST SERVANT.

Why art thou out this weather, lord of hen-roosts?

GONARDO.

Because I can't get in. Where hangs the gate?

SECOND SERVANT.

Where thou wouldst now be hanging, master Crow,
Had every man his meed. Whose coop hast robbed to-night?

THIRD SERVANT.

Yes, sirrah, whose?
Hold up the lightning's lantern to your face,
And look in ours and swear you're honest man.

GONARDO.

Where hangs the gate, I pray you?

THIRD SERVANT.

Call you that praying, every word an oath?

GONARDO.

I do beseech you tell me.

THIRD SERVANT.

Imprecate not.

GONARDO.

Kind gentlemen,—

THIRD SERVANT.

Abuse us not; for we
Are all cats' sons, so see thee best i' the dark.
We have sharp claws, too:—sirrah, put your back down.—
It is not raining: 'tis you spitting at us.

GONARDO.

Assist me hence.   I do implore you, tell me
Where stands the gate.

SECOND SERVANT.

Against its post.

GONARDO.

Where that ?

SECOND SERVANT.

I'the earth.

GONARDO.

Aside.] Plagues pester them !   [*Aloud.*] Good gentlemen, I stand
Craving for gate or post : pray you be moved.

THIRD SERVANT.

Stand there, most excellent post, and be reproved.

SECOND SERVANT.

Yes, be improved.

GONARDO.

I grow much better, sirs.

THIRD SERVANT.

Take root, take root, toe deep into the ground ;
This rain will make thee mount amazingly.

GONARDO.

You are too hard.

FOURTH SERVANT.

No swearing, such a night :
It were a very fatal night to swear in.

GONARDO.

How your tongues wag to-night !   It might be raining
Wine, not cold water.

THIRD SERVANT.

Lie not : it is warm ;
Aired, sir.   This torrent falls like warmed ripe ale ;
Comes creamed by whipping winds, and through it roaring
The red-hot plunging pokers of the lightnings.
Thou hast not drunk our healths.

GONARDO (*aside*).
     Diseases take them!
Aloud.] Heaven bless you all, my masters!—Once again,
Where hangs the gate.

SECOND SERVANT.
    Just where it did this morning.

GONARDO.
Pray you, no longer mock me: which way thither?

THIRD SERVANT.
Down by the river, up by the rill,
Close by the currant-bush, round by the mill;
Next through the holme, sir, and over the stile,
Past the old haunted house, eighth of a mile;
Then look round about you, and straight you shall see
Whate'er you may want, sir,—if there it shall be.
A dish of due directions; plums, sir, chew them.
      [*Exeunt* SERVANTS, *laughing.*

GONARDO.
Even by their fruits, men still we know them.
How luckless, lost in this entangling labyrinth!
It was the Prince went by: I know his foot.
Along; though dark the night, and these wet walks,
Intricate as are the winding ways of woman.—
One comes this way.
    [*Exit, and enter the* PRINCE, *disguised as a* MONK.

HYLAS.
Hist, hist, Volina, is it thou?—hist, hist.
      [*Exit, and enter* FILIPPO.

FILIPPO.
What need of whispering have the innocent?
'Tis she and her prim paramour. What matters
Rain?—lust is like the old Greek fire that burned
In water best. They are not seething, but
Red-hot, in this deep drench.—I see them there.
   [*Exit, and re-enter presently at another place, with drawn sword.*

FILIPPO.

Still will I follow !—though she be to me
Dead, yet the man who killed her with his kindness,
Must, for the debt incurred in her dishonor,
Even at the bank and counter of these grounds
Pay down his life. Down faster, skyey flood,
And wash this hand from foul seducer's blood.

[*Exit, and enter* VOLINA *from the opposite direction.*

VOLINA.

Why do I start at any sound to-night,
When nature seems one vast, loud-raving ghost;
Or, seized with throes of mortal agony,
Flash lightnings in her dying eyes, while thunder
Draws the death-rattle in the welkin's throat ?
Again that sound !   Oh, should it be my lord !
It must, it must : methinks I hear his voice
Chiding.   A clash of swords,—oh, shielding heavens !
Should Hylas fall a victim to his vengeance ;
Or should himself, i'the darkness, fatal fall
By Hylas' ignorant hand !—Oh, no, no, no :
It was the tempest's tongue, not Filippo's ;
That sound was but the battle of the boughs.
And now 't has ceased.—Ah, well, 't has ceased, for yet
My heart not ceases tremble, nor my limbs ;
Nor sudden dew to ooze upon my brow,
Drawn from my marrow to the clammy verge,—
And now returning cold and creeping back,
As back the skulking blood creeps from my heart.
Oh, coward, coward, coward am I now !
How am I changed since only yesternight ;
How am I altered, once so careless, bold ;
How have I eaten of the fatal tree
Of knowledge !   Nature, too, appears
To have partaken with me : 'tis all eyes,
All ears ; all watching, all accusing me ;
All waiting to bear witness to my husband.

Yet all without's but shade of what's within:
These sounds are nothing but my guilty self,
That finds unfriendly life in every leaf.
Still, opportune as terrible this tempest.
Tempest, grow louder, riot in the air;
Darken and deepen, so that I may glide
(As into chaos hell-escaping ghost)
Unheard, unseen, with all my guilt upon me,
From here with Hylas to I know not where.
Come, Hylas, fetch me from yon forfeit roof,
Back, wandering wife, back, wasting, weary woman;
Thence go where'er thy ruiner may set thee,
Poor painted target for the shot of time.

[*Going, when occurs a more terrible flash of lightning and peal of thunder.*

Oh, Heaven, aim not at me all thy volleys!
Shoot not thy forky tongue so near me, lightning;
Bully me not, big thunder; nor, sharp wind,
So cruel scourge me: I have not wronged ye,—
Nor thee, hurled hail, stone-casting Pharisee.

[*Exit, and re-enter* FILIPPO, *sheathing his sword.*

FILIPPO.

A glimpse o'the moon were well. Sword, get to bed;
Thoud'st nearly done mad murder in the dark.
How like the prince's the fence o'the flying fool!—
Lo, yonder stalks another! Follow:—no,
It is my purblind fancy, that mistakes
Trees for men walking. Horror walks the night,
So dark, so dismal, and so weirdly wild,
With such a bellowing broil of elements,
Within the dormitory of the sky,
That not a star dares peep from out its lids,
As little ones whose parents fiercely quarrel.
Hast thou a quarrel, night, with nature? then
Straight cast her out, as I shall my false wife.
If day have wronged thee, overthrow her lamp,—
Scatter her embers o'er the shameful hearth,—
Be the sole tenant of this world-house dark.—

Oh, how this phrase might well befit myself!
It is my sole house now, this wide, dark world.
Yonder is not my house, fast darkening now:
I was cast out when they cast out mine honor.
I must approach it when all lights are out;
Mine eyes will glare enough. Volina, girl,
We would not strike thee blind with o'ermuch light;
Not, blasting, blind thee with our gloomy glance:—
Oh, no, let love turn half its fire askance.   [*Exit.*

SCENE V.

The hall of FILIPPO's *mansion.* HYLAS, *disguised as a monk;* VOLINA
leaning on his arm, and weeping bitterly. Time, midnight.

VOLINA.

My heart will break, even yet; my heart will break!
Would that it might; would, would I now might die!—
But guilt is hardier than innocence:
The wicked live to bear long years of woe.

HYLAS.

Your servants will return, and we are lost.
This is not well, this is not well, Volina.
Your household, or abed or sent abroad,
Deliver you into the hands o'the time,
That cries with opportunity, "begone!"
Succumb not in the crisis. But one step,
And you have crossed the ridge; to walk, concealed,
Adown the other side. Take your farewell;
But, while you mourn that thus you leave these halls,
Mourn more for that you ever entered them.

VOLINA.

Farewell, my home; farewell, farewell, my lord;
Farewell now, my domestics, that at morn
May seek but shall not find me. With scared eyes,
Soon must they meet their master, and to stone
Turn him with Gorgon news.   [*Enter* FILIPPO.

HYLAS.

What man art thou?

FILIPPO.

A stranger, who, in homeless misery,
Seeks shelter from the chaos of this night.

HYLAS.

Thou canst not harbour here.

FILIPPO.

Why not?—I will.

HYLAS.

Beggar, begone; hie hence unto the town.
Here's money for thy lodging and thy cheer.

FILIPPO.

Withdraw that hand, or I may bite it off;
So hungry am I, famished, foolish, fierce.

HYLAS.

Thou hast more fire than famine in thine eye.—
Madman, avaunt!

FILIPPO.

Who told you I was mad?
[*Attempting to seize Hylas.*
Thou stony bosom, off with that monk's hood:
Thou art not of the charitable tribe.
Doff me that gown, that doth conceal the devil,
And shew thee hideous, damned, undominoed.—
What is there sacred in a stolen stole?

HYLAS.

Approach me not, but to our monastery.
'Tis the Blackfriars; there thou mayst be lodged.
The way is short. Begone; thou canst not miss it:
Nor I be stayed, who to a soul have come
That needs especial unction.

FILIPPO.

Liar! Fiend,
May thine own sulphur choke thee!—Quick, or ere

K

I strangle thee ; as Hercules the snakes
That stole into his cradle, as thou'st stolen
Into mine honor.—Quick ; or this nerved arm,
As powerful now as that of Hercules,
When, with his hands, he tore the Nemean lion,
May yet tear thee.   Off with that cowl and robe ;
Unfrock thee, lest my sword should strike thee, fatal
As Perseus' when he smote the salt-sea monster
That came devour Andromeda o'er the wave.
Ah, we would kill thee now, but, thee destroyed,
There were no fiend to terrify the bad.

HYLAS.

What would'st thou, man ?   Wild maniac, what mean'st thou ?
Profanest wretch, avaunt ! nor still defraud
The dying of his craved viaticum ;
Lest, in thine agony, thyself should'st lack.
Impostor, hence.

FILIPPO.
We're no impostor.

HYLAS.
Hence !
Shall death bear off a spirit unannealed,
Poised on the whitening shore of pallid lips ;
Whence it can only whisper wafts of faith
Into mine open ear, while thou dost blow
Out the long gale of thine importunate breath ?

FILIPPO.

I cannot slay thee,—though it were no murder.—
But, storm, hast, listening, held so long thy peace,
While we have vainly brabbled ?   Speak now, roar ;
Churn up this house' foundations as a flood,
And drown therein this woman and this man !

HYLAS.
Away !—no more of this.

VOLINA.
Away, good man.

FILIPPO.

Away, adultress, if thou would'st not yet
See killed this unknown villain.   Cling not to him ;
Or, in my fury, I may kill e'en thee.

VOLINA.

'Tis Filippo !

FILIPPO.

Ay, Filippo, dost know me ?—
Tremble, thou guilty ; strive to hide thyself,—
Yea, strive to hide thy head, as doth the ostrich
When it is chased by the Arabian.
Girl, fly while vengeance on this villain stays me.
To HYLAS.] Wilt not disclose thee ?   Thus, then,—

[*Draws his sword ; and, at the same moment, enter a* COURTIER, *with Officers of Justice.*

Ah ! who ye,
And what your errand ?

COURTIER.

Servants of the Duke,
Upon whose warrant you are each arrested ;
Thou, stranger, being suspected as a spy,
These two because it is Tremohla's will,
And instant all must with me to the palace.

FILIPPO.

Then am I cheated for awhile :—no matter.
I willingly accept your custody,
Since, with me, likewise, you convey these two,
Who shall be charged with gravest misdemeanour.

[HYLAS *whispers to the* COURTIER

Strip that vile minister of hell, not heaven ;
Uncloak him for me.—Oh, religion, what
A cloak hast thou not oft been made for sin ;
That hath encased himself in thine attire,
And stalked with ostentation through the world,
Receiving bow and homage, till thyself
Hast been regarded with suspicious eyes !
Off with his borrowed badges, tear them from him :

He is no monk, not he ; but he is what
I will not style him till before the Duke.
Respect you not his cowl, (all of the monk
He hath,) for all beneath is villainy.

HYLAS.

Heed him not, pray you, since it is a madman,
That even now hath entered as you see him ;
And said such wild things, with such wild demeanour,
As stamp him what I say he is,—mad, mad.

COURTIER.

You all must straight appear before the Duke.

HYLAS.

Then, lady, come, since it e'en must be so.
I will not leave you, be I monk or no.

[*Exeunt omnes.*

SCENE VI.

A Room of State in the Palace. The DUKE, *enthroned on a dais, surrounded by* LORDS, SENATORS, COURTIERS, *and others. Before him* FILIPPO, HYLAS, VOLINA, *and* GONARDO. *Time now past midnight.*

DUKE.

It is our worthy servant, Filippo !
No trait of travel, no disguise, no grief,
Can make us strange unto those lineaments.
Be of good cheer, dear Filippo :
We will avenge thee on whoe'er it may,
Advancing justice to the very verge
O' the balance, till it overweigh thy black
And heavy wrong.   We have arrested thee
'Midst thy soul's riot, as the parent plucks
Out of the mob-filled street his darling child,
Retaining it in doors ; but more to prove
Ourselves thy quick avenger.   Woe to him
That hath abused thine absence ! woe to him
That hath (as the Saul-bidden witch of Endor

Once brought old Samuel up from Hades) brought me
Trembling to sit on this midnight tribunal!
Whoso hath injured thee, one step from here
Shall bring within his pale of punishment.
Swift, we await to hear from thine own tongue
What brings thee back in this sore plight from Arno.

FILIPPO.

That I am wronged, and in what tender part,
Your highness knows, else why am I thus here?
Then all I ask you is to unmask my wronger,
(Who, I believe, now stands beneath that cowl,)
And yield him to my punitory sword.
But for the other who hath wronged me most,
Mine own right hand, all that therein I seek
Is the poor liberty to cut it off.

DUKE.

Uncloak thyself, monk, if thou beest such;
And, for the lady, let her still be covered,—
We would not wantonly up-conjure blushes,
For which, we hope, there is no guilty cause.

[HYLAS *casts off his monk's disguise.*

DUKE.

Hylas? oh, heavens! Hylas? oh, God!

FILIPPO.

Now dost thou press too heavily upon
Me, fate! Hylas, and is it thou? Oh, oh,
Him for whose weal I laboured to this last.—
Let me begone, for I am helpless here:
How can I strike my prince?—Oh, my dear master,
How can I strike your false, deceitful son?

DUKE.

My son? no son of mine; a bastard surely:—
And, yet, how much of me his form contains
This deed bears witness. Now requital comes;
Inexorable is the hand of Heaven:—
But 't should have stricken wider, not so near.
Speak, thou delinquent; speak, oh, speak thy shame.

HYLAS.

What shall be rendered, what shall be adduced,
To this dread accusation, save that all
Was love ?
I saw his lady, and, if I adored her,
It was no more than he himself had done.—
And I was young,—and is not she young too ?
Oh, think upon our youth and great temptation !
Yet one there is, that damned Gallantio,
The great, original tempter to this sin,
Who, if no place in hell be hot enough
(And I aver there is not) for his crimes,
Let him be given me this hour to torture.
But for this angel who with me hath slidden,—
Not fallen, for she clings still to the sky,—
So far she from the Tophet of pollution,
As to raise me into the Empyrean,
Behold no power on earth (and Heaven will drop
A tear to wash out what towards it is wrong)
Shall cause me to resign her or cease cherish.

DUKE.

Thou art mine own again, thou art mine own !

FILIPPO.

My wrath grows sick ; revenge within me dies.

HYLAS.

What yet thou harbourest direct on me :—
Yet spare me for the sake of her thou sparest,
And who hath not been more by me beset,
Than all beleaguered by unnatural custom,
Which basely bargains where it ought to woo,
And drives the lamb home that it ought to lead.
Oh, much her fault hath to extenuate it.
Didst not thou bargain for her, Filippo,
As might'st thou bargain for a beauteous mare,
Or treat for statue to adorn thy hall ?
Herein her destiny scarce better than

That of the purchased, poor Circassian,
By parents sold to arms of amorous Turk.
True, thou so generous appearedst to her,
She went with thee, thine unresisting slave;
But with her person thou boughtest not her heart,
Unpurchaseable, as thou shouldst have known,
Ungiveable, else had she given it thee.

FILIPPO.

I give her back, all that remains to me
Of her, whom I had thought to love for life;
Yea, whom I love, and must love till I die.
If I did purchase her, I, unredeemed,
Relinquish; if I did entice, restore.
I see mine error, also feel my fine,—
Loss of myself along with loss of her.
Had I recalled our age's disparity,—
Remembered that, while she was at the foot,
I trod the landing of ascending years,—
This had not been: but now too late I learn
That nature doth, in time as well as kind,
Abhor the hybrid, still doth cast it off;
That youth must youth attract, as drop does drop;
That souls commune not for that forms are wed,
No more than oil and water mix, up-pent.
Life's various stages, toward each other, are
As foreign, though as fellow, travellers,—
Strangers on road and at sojourning inn,—
Unlike of thought, of unfamiliar tongue.—
Stern lesson this to learn; hard, hard to bear
This burning balsam to my wound's wide fissure.
Yet were the dagger which destroys less cruel,
Not wielded by a prince whom I have loved,
And in this latest instance thought to serve,
Perhaps mistakenly.—I say no more,
Ungrateful prince, thou friend-forgetting Hylas,
But thou mayst give to me that cloak and cowl,
For to the Blackfriars now in sooth I wend;

Thither retire from life and public care,
Cast off my honors as I shall this dress,
Assume the shroud of sorrow, and be buried
Out of this withered world, and be no more
Known as Count Filippo the minister,
But as the sad-eyed friar in his weeds.

GONARDO.

Not thuswise, Filippo; not thus my neighbour.

FILIPPO.

Ah, is it you? I did not see you, sir.
They told me you were dead.

GONARDO.

               So was I lately,
But have arisen; still, should you be buried,
I'll be interred too, having greater need.

FILIPPO.

Are you, too, stricken? Can Pereza hold
A living wight more dead at root than I?

GONARDO.

More deeply wronged am I, Count Filippo,
Than you are, I who have not given cause
Unto my wronger, my false wife, as you;
Yet am I not so wronged as you are, since
That which I lose was ne'er worth half your prize.

DUKE.

He speaks in riddles.—Are there two of you,
Coming like usurous Jews to ruin me,—
Ruin old Tremohla for his spendthrift son?
My days are numbered:—take, yes, take my life.

          [*The* DUKE *sinks, but is supported by others.*

HYLAS.

There is another, be he quickly brought;—
But tie my hands, lest they of vengeance cheat
Gonardo's, who, if knew he all I know
Touching Gallantio, whom now we summon,

Would, at his sight, be prompted to destroy him,—
Have turned his fingers into lion's claws.

GONARDO.

I've ta'en account of him : he has been seized,
And with him greater felon.

A SENATOR.

Here he comes ;—
And with him one uncalled for, even your wife.

[*Enter* GALLANTIO *and* PAPHIANA *in custody.*

GONARDO.

Oh, thou vile woman !

PAPHIANA.

Oh, sir, is that you ?
Your letters lied, then :—but you must be dead :
Yet never did I see such dark-skinned corpse.

HYLAS.

Where and how did you find them ?

OFFICER (*in charge of them*).

At her house ;
And, for the manner, even as we blush
To tell your highness.

HYLAS (*to* GALLANTIO).

Lucifer is light
As is the morning-star, compared with thee.
Turn him this way.   Look on me, hideous villain.

GALLANTIO (*gazing at* FILIPPO).

I have a more inviting prospect there.

HYLAS.

Oh, thou consummate fiend, how hast thou triumphed !
How, but to satisfy a private grudge,
(For which, at morn, thou find'st a shameful death,)
Hast thou committed a wide public wrong ;
Sweeping myself, Volina, Filippo,
Into thy malice' yawn !

PAPHIANA.

And is she fallen !
Is she indeed, then, laid as low as I ?—
Oh, oh, my lady, you may well seem grave.

GALLANTIO.

How sober Filippo looks ! how exile-like !
Is he just banished ?   Shall he row with me
Old Charon's galley o'er the Styx to-morrow,
For that you have conspired my death I know ?

FILIPPO.

What means he, that he points his gibes at me ?
Can any tell me ?   Wherefore is he here ?

HYLAS.

He tempted me to the attempt.

FILIPPO.

                       No more :
I see it all.

GALLANTIO.

           Thank Heaven thou dost ;
Then there is not one drop of vengeance lost.

HYLAS.

Take him away : he shall no longer gloat
Upon his victim, nor offend mine eyes.
Straight to the rack with him ; not to extort
Confession, for that were a needless task,
But that Gonardo, who should ply the engine,
May wreak his wrath on his offending form.
Goad him ; yet not too hard, lest he expire
Too soon,—so cheat the multitude at morn,
Who hate him, too, for his low ravages.

GALLANTIO.

But do not let that odious Filippo
Serve even thus your highness.—You, Gonardo,
I neither hate nor fear.   Oft have I used,
But never loved, your wife ; your fortune, too,
Some little, so repay you in my blood,
Drop, if you will, by drop.   I am content
To die, losing by piecemeal, should it please you,
My flesh, having fleshed my hatred on that man.

FILIPPO.

Nay, let him live, Gonardo : equal parts
Own we in yon foul forfeit.   Let him live,
And to the galleys go.

HYLAS.

We that forbid :
He shall behold the light of day no more.
Let him all night lie in a heated vault ;
That he may think, ere death, he is in hell.
His conscience shall be to him the grim devil.

GALLANTIO.

No easier doom I'd wish :—you cannot scare
Me.   As the salamander, cast in fire,
Exudes preserving mucus, so my mind,
Cased in thick satisfaction of success,
Shall be uninjured ; and my well-worn body,
So fed, so full, so surfeited, with pleasure,
It cannot murmur should it end in pain.
I am asbestus to your furnace rage :
You cannot melt, though you may burn or break me.
Give me my portion.—Lo, the Duke is dead.
He was a man, were he alive and young,
Would not have pierced his pander,—was a lion
Whose paws had stroked his jackal, lieu of strangled.

HYLAS.

Away with him : he doth too long insult us.—
Oh, now, my father, you have passed away ;
Nor stayed to sorrow o'er this tragedy,
Whereof the argument, I fear, is thine ;—
Thou, who didst seek to wed me in hot haste,
To compensate for thine own tardy marriage,
Which thou, by amours cooled, too long delayed.
Volina, look upon those lineaments.
None loved you more than he, departed now ;
None more desired to see you at this court,
Whereof, had you not been our minister's wife,
You should have been the Duchess.—Sir, forgive me :
I had forgot your presence.

FILIPPO.

Mind not that;
Remember me not now: I would forget
All, if I could; I would forget that I,
In marrying her, have wronged her even as much
As she hath me.   Within a monastery
I'll pray, if Heaven assist this broken heart,
For you and her; say masses for the spirit
Of the dead Duke, and strive forgive all souls
That ever injured me,—even thee, Gallantio.

HYLAS.

Is he not yet withdrawn ?

FILIPPO.

Pray, let him live.

GALLANTIO.

Take me away !—he will not curse me.—Curse,
Fool, curse me.   [GALLANTIO *is led out.*

A LORD.

He is vulnerable, though
He thought himself in stronger panoply
Than armadillo's mail.

A COURTIER.

This feathery shaft,
Forgiveness, falling lighter than the snow-flake,
Hath pierced the hedgehog; when the javelin
Of threats had failed.

GONARDO.

Forgiveness' point is sharp;
'T has found and entered him between the joints.
Filippo, you on earth have found him hell,
For coals of fire now flame upon his head.

FILIPPO.

May they but purge him, or refine what's left
Within his breast of manhood; for his time
Is short for meeting his eternal doom.—
And now let me depart.   Hereafter, friends,
When you shall tell the tale of Filippo,

Say sudden ended with dire accident,
Even in the midst o'the pageant, his career;
Say that he sinned,—say, too, how he was punished.
Going]. I leave my good and evil with you. Now
Seek Filippo no more : he grants no favors,
No private audience,—no more holds levee,
No more frequents the court ; but humbly goes
Prepare him for the court o'the King of kings.
No child I have, no heir ; mine ancient title
(Which is a bauble I ne'er played with much)
Goes to a scion of another name,
With the hereditary, rich estates.
Thus, lightened much, I go to the Blackfriars,
There to devise a moiety of what rests
Unto the Church ; bequeathing the remainder
(After some trifling legacies and gifts)
To the three sisters of my secretary.
To VOLINA.] Your marriage portion you shall have returned ;
With aught you may request of me besides,
As being yours by right of others' gift,
Or of your cunning fingers' workmanship.
All I request is your own miniature,
That you did give me on our wedding-day.

HYLAS.
It shall be yours.

FILIPPO.
Asks she not aught from me ?

HYLAS.
Vex her not now with questions, Filippo :
Her heart is all too full of working grief.
Lo, as a full-charged flask, for want of air
Doth stubbornly refuse to void its contents,
So do her lips refuse to yield her thoughts.

FILIPPO (*going*).
Then let us part in silence.

VOLINA.
Oh, no, no :—
One thing I ask, one only thing,—forgiveness.

FILIPPO.

That I have granted you already, ere
You asked it.   Grant the same to me.

HYLAS.

She hath.—
Gonardo, you have mine for the spy's part
That you have played herein.—What say you now
To your awaiting and unfaithful wife?

GONARDO.

Nothing,—but that the harvest in her womb
Knows not my husbandry.

PAPHIANA.

Can you affirm it?

GONARDO.

Most truly, madam; and such evidence
Hath been adduced, this night, of your deep guilt,
As shall obtain for me swift separation.

PAPHIANA.

Take it.   You will return my dower, as he
Hath hers returned to his frail partner.

A SENATOR.

No word for thine associate in dishonor,—
Poor, sunken wretch, that hath gone down for ever?

PAPHIANA.

Let him disgorge the ducats from me drained :—
But they would be my lord's, there.

GONARDO.

Paphiana,
Thine hate and scorn, like two king's-evidence,
Treacherously drag thy guilt before the court.
'Tis well thou art so guilty none may doubt it,—
Well, thine effrontery doth magnify,
As with a microscope, thy fall; else I
Might have been counted a mere jealous fool.

PAPHIANA.

Oh, you were sick, sir, were you?—dying, dead?
You patrolled past my threshold; stood near, keeping

Guard like a grenadier in the street,
While we were making merry in the parlour.
Oh, oh.

HYLAS.

No more of this : bear to a couch that corse,
And let it lie in state.—Oh, now the state
Falls upon too weak shoulders. Father, this last blow,
Striking thee down, hath struck the scaffolding
Away from me, before I am well built ;—
Hath stricken you away, Count Filippo,
Ingratitude towards whom in this last act,
As thing corrupt dropped into a deep fount,
Hath poisoned all my stream of future years.
Forgive me ere you go, if I dare ask you ;
Let me not be beyond your mercy's pale.

FILIPPO.

I that have all forgiven, shall I not
Forgive, then, thee ?—yea, for his sake who lies,
After the storm and winter of his days,
There like a snow-drift spread across the throne,
Scroll and compendium of mortality.
Hylas, believe resentment may not rest
With whomsoever seeketh to be saved :
Malice for demons and the souls o'the lost.
We thee forgive, as we would be forgiven.

HYLAS.

Oh, make me not to lose now self-possession !—
Enough, enough.—What now remains, save each
To take his sober way, and meditate
On this sad scene ! Judge me not harshly, lords,
Nor cover aught in mine offence deformed :
But, oh, let this catastrophe appal ;
Let manhood waste no more its lusty days,
In vain, voluptuous celibacy ;
Nor let those dream whose life's hot summer's past
Without a wedded partner, to renew
Their vernal season in their issue's spring.—

And now convey that corse from here.   Move slow
On sorrow's foot.—Volina, let us go.

VOLINA.

We go, but different ways, toward different ends:
You to a throne in a luxurious court,
I to a cell amongst severest nuns ;
Wherein, if penitence can pierce the skies,
The dew of pardon on me may descend,
E'en for the sake of that heaven-opening blood
Was shed on Calvary for such as I ;
Whose portion else had been the fallen's pit.—
May you escape it likewise.

HYLAS.

We are contrite !—

Though, late and little, our contrition shows
As tardy trickling from a summer rill.
Our eyes are dry as brooks in dusty summer.
Perplexed at heart, upon our lips the words
Lie bound, as running rills by winter's frost;—
But do not thou flow hence.   Stay : we may still
Make some rude restitution,—yet retain
Thee in the bound and prospect of our view.
But, oh, to see thee from our sight recede
Into the deep, dim vista of the veil,
Not called thereto by nature !   Here abide ;—
Or, if thou must retire to votive shades,
Here found an order of pale penitents,
Whose sisters shall be queens and noble dames,—
Fair frail ones whom the foul fiend once beset,
But who may bloom as angels yet on high.—
But thou dost mock us with that glimmering smile.
Too saintly sad thy look.   Thy solemn eyes
Droop dolefully as two mist-setting stars ;
From thine, shed darkness o'er our sinking soul.
Thy soul is set; we see it in thine eye :
Then what remains but here to abdicate,—
Descend, indeed, before we have arisen,—

With crucifix go pace the cloistered aisle,
Instead of sitting, sceptred, on a throne?
We will betake us to the sackcloth, too,
Who should have donned the purple,—shave the crown,
Now covered with these Absalom-like locks,
That should be covered with Pereza's crown.
Tremohla sought fair Arno's crown for me;
On Arno's head Pereza's crown now be.

[*Curtain falls.*

THE END.